LIVES OF GREAT RELIGIOUS BOOKS

Dietrich Bonhoeffer's
Letters and Papers from Prison

LIVES OF GREAT RELIGIOUS BOOKS

Dietrich Bonhoeffer's
Letters and Papers from Prison

A BIOGRAPHY

Martin E. Marty

PRINCETON UNIVERSITY PRESS

Princeton and Oxford

Published by Princeton University Press, 41 William Street,
Princeton, New Jersey 08540
In the United Kingdom: Princeton University Press, 6 Oxford Street,
Woodstock, Oxfordshire OX20 1TW

press.princeton.edu

Library of Congress Cataloging-in-Publication Data

Marty, Martin E., 1928–
   Dietrich Bonhoeffer's letters and papers from prison : a biography /
Martin E. Marty.
      p.   cm. — (Lives of great religious books)
   Includes bibliographical references and index.
   ISBN 978-0-691-13921-0 (hardcover : alk. paper)
   1. Bonhoeffer, Dietrich, 1906–1945. 2. Bonhoeffer, Dietrich,
1906–1945. Widerstand und Ergebung. 3. Prisoners of war—
Germany—Correspondence. 4. Theologians—Germany—
Correspondence. I. Title.
   BX4827.B57M359 2011
   230'.044092—dc22
   [B]   2010029618

British Library Cataloging-in-Publication Data is available

Jacket photograph: Prison cell in Tegel; archival photo

This book has been composed in Garamond Premier Pro
Printed on acid-free paper. ∞
Printed in the United States of America
10 9 8 7 6 5 4 3 2 1

To John de Gruchy and Victoria J. Barnett

and in memory of Eberhard Bethge

CONTENTS

Figure 4 is in the Ullstein Biederdienst collection; all other figures are from archival collections, now widely available

ACKNOWLEDGMENTS

John de Gruchy, Victoria J. Barnett, and Michael West made available the page proofs of volume 8 of the Dietrich Bonhoeffer Works (DBWE), *Letters and Papers from Prison* (Minneapolis, 2010). It was therefore possible for me to convert translations and references in my first draft, from the 1971 edition, which had become standard in the English-speaking world. That 1971 version was subtitled "New Greatly Enlarged Edition," but the one being published in 2010 and referenced here is "newer" and "more greatly enlarged"—double the size of the 1971 edition—and will become and remain the new standard scholarly reference. The extensive quotations from this edition appear by permission of Fortress. I am indebted to many members of the International Bonhoeffer Society, which hosted the Martys at the Tenth. International Prague Congress in 2008, and where John Matthews, president of the English Language Section of the International Bonhoeffer Society, was our guide.

I was able to converse about Bonhoeffer and the subject of this book with veterans in the project, especially Clifford Green, chairman of the DBWE editorial board; Geffrey Kelly, a veteran, now emeritus, on the board; translators Martin Rumscheidt and Nancy Lukens; and many more. I have been reading Bonhoeffer since 1953 and writing on him on occasion since 1962, but Prague was the first time I could meet with the larger company of the custodians of Bonhoefferiana and scholars who have long influenced me. John de Gruchy, our sometime host in South Africa, did much to tutor me in the ways of interpreting the Bonhoeffer Letters and Papers, and he deserves special thanks. Two unnamed readers for Princeton University Press made valuable suggestions. Fred Appel, who invented the series of which this book is an early product, was of great help at all stages along the way. I also thank Harriet Julia Marty for her generous and loving participation in the times of travel, research, writing, and now publication.

—M.E.M.

Dietrich Bonhoeffer's
Letters and Papers from Prison

A BIOGRAPHY

The Birth of a Book

An old photograph provides a glimpse into a dismal cell at a Nazi prison called Tegel. Wan light falls in from a tiny window that is too high for a prisoner to use to take in a landscape, but one who is alert and sensitive might glimpse the upper branches of a high tree or a low hanging cloud, and through that opening, hear a thrush. A standard-issue plank bed with a blanket drawn tight over it takes up most of the small space in the cell and in the picture, and a board to which one could attach notices is on the unadorned wall. Other furnishings are sparse. We know from other sources than the photograph of the presence of a nearby stool and a bucket, positioned for we-all-know-what. Guards, who were forbidden to talk to prisoners, could peer in through a slot in the door to view the inmate, who could not see out. Visitors today can still imagine something of what it must have been like for a captive to squirm or pace in its ten-foot by seven-foot floor space.

All the senses can come into play during such imagining. For instance, the odor of the whole third floor in which this cell 92 stood, the prisoner's pen for a year and a half, was barely endurable. No smell of fresh soap offered a contrast that could render the atmosphere slightly bearable, because there was not any soap available that could have helped make living with one's own odors less than dreadful.

The Birthplace of the Book

From that cramped space designed to kill creativity and bury hope, however, there issued letters and papers that became the substance of one of the great testimonial books of the twentieth century. Since there is so little to observe in the shadowed picture of this room, we are left other reminders and, later, his words written there, to fill it in with a human portrait, that of the author. He was Dietrich Bonhoeffer, the best-known German Protestant pastor, who resisted Hitler and paid for his actions and expressions with his life. He was a man of many paradoxes: a longtime pacifist, something that Lutherans were not supposed to be; an *inconsistent* pacifist who became a conspirator in an assassination plot against Adolf Hitler; a thinker who took citizenship seriously but technically was guilty of treason; a still young world traveler who did his most memorable work in this cramping cell.

Many who view the photo of this enclosure do so knowing in advance from his writing and that of his friends something of what was occurring in his mind and in the cell. His letters tell us, but in any case it is not difficult to conjure up a sense of what his aloneness meant to the confined man, who was a naturally gregarious and friendly sort. For a time he was unspoken to, even by guards. In his first days there they tossed in his meager breakfasts. They were forbidden to recognize the humanity of such a locked-in person. We learn from a letter that succumbing to despair was tempting to the prisoner and that at a low moment suicide was even an option, because he considered himself to be "basically" dead.[1] We learn that, instead of killing himself, he began to write, especially as his material circumstances eventually, if only slightly, improved. Many of his notes, of course, were personal letters, some passed on through authorities and some smuggled out and then transmitted to his best friend, Pastor Eberhard Bethge, who saved them. No publisher would have seen a potentially attractive book in the letters or his other various jottings, musings, and poems written in prison.

During the dark nights of loneliness and in the bleak mornings there cannot have been much incentive for the letter-writer to greet the day from amid the sounds of silence at times and, at others, from the din of noises made by prisoners and guards. Yet, against all odds, a book was being drafted. After World War II, Eberhard Bethge, who had hidden the scraps and scribblings in the days of danger, evaluated and organized them. This meant deciphering scripts and arranging pages to fashion the book that the English-speaking world knows as Dietrich Bonhoeffer, *Letters and Papers from Prison*. Issuing from that seventy-square-foot cell, this little work came to be known, read, and used around the world well into a new century. While the physical setting of its letters and papers was a place capable of inducing claustrophobia, spiritually these contents served readers everywhere as a testimony to openness, possibility, and hope.

Many letters and thus many pages of the eventual book dealt with rather ordinary matters. But surrounding the chatty items that make the letters personally attractive were theological reflections that, Bethge was to decide, might appeal to and serve the church, the university, and the traumatized but recovering nation. After Bonhoeffer's execution as the European war was ending, Bethge did some tentative and exploratory disseminating of some of the writings. The positive reaction, at first from a close circle of friends, turned out to be part of a test that taught Bethge to observe that many readers *were* welcoming this genre. They were becoming involved at second hand with the life and witness of this different kind of theologian, Bonhoeffer.

The Inner Life of the Book

Readers indicated that they wanted to read more examples of the informal, personal, and concrete witness written from within the prison contexts. They longed to have revealed to them the yearnings and hopes of the still young author. For an example: whoever knew Bonhoeffer personally was aware of his esthetic interests. He would write about music even when he was not able to hear much of it. He even used musical metaphors to describe his life: at base was the *cantus firmus* that faith provided, so he was able to live life polyphonically.[2] This short reference has often been picked up on by others who were emotionally far removed from his prison experiences, and it became a theme in their spiritual disciplines.

Along with music, to the end Bonhoeffer wrote and read poetry, but he won no points from his young fiancée, Maria von Wedemeyer, who received a letter in which he dismissed Rainer Maria von Rilke, the major poet of the times, whom she cherished. Mention of a fiancée leads to the topic of Bonhoeffer's yearnings, reflected in the amorous longings, expressed discreetly, by a passionate author who could restrain only some of his ardor. Naturally, evidences of all this were treated fondly by his friend, editor Bethge. Reports of one instance in which the imprisoned Bonhoeffer and his fiancée stole an embrace during her rare, brief, and guarded visit at Tegel prison are moving, but one can find such stories in the celebrity press, and the Bonhoeffer letters do not provide titillation. Their author did tend to his romance, writing that he hoped that he and his Maria would stay on the same wavelength, but he did admit to some friction, which was quite natural, given the couple's circumstances. Maria made clear in her letters that physical presence was something for which she yearned. Moving as the stories of the romance are, they would not have been distinctive enough to warrant publication in isolation. It was not until decades had passed and after Maria's death that her own letters were published.

The letters and papers from prison reveal much about Bonhoeffer's spiritual life and vocation, and these served a new generation of collegians and seminarians who were looking for models of witness and courage. They tell of his spiritual life and vocation, as for instance in the first letter, when Bonhoeffer asked his friend, who had served as his pastor back when they were studying theology and pastoral practice together, now, through letters, again to be his pastor, since he had not been allowed to see one in prison. He pleaded to his friend: "After so many long months without worship, confession and the Lord's Supper and without *consolation fratrum*—[be] my pastor once more, as you have so often been in the past, and listen to me." Then came a revelation about Bonhoeffer's psyche: "You are the only person who knows that '*acedia*,' '*tristitia*' [sadness in the face of spiritual good, medievalists called it] with all its ominous consequences, has often haunted me." But, he resolved, "neither human beings nor the devil" would prevail.[3]

The voice of conscience was also whispered in the letters. At first, wrote Bonhoeffer, he had wondered "whether it was really for the cause of Christ" that he was leading Eberhard and all the others to experience so much grief. And we hear the language of resolve: "I soon put that out of my head as a temptation, as I became certain that the duty had been laid on me to hold out in this boundary situation with all its problems; I became quite content to do this, and have remained so ever since (I Peter 2:20; 3:14)."[4]

Sometimes personal events mentioned in the letters help one understand the whole ensuing editorial venture. Thus, back on April 4, 1943, the spring of the engagements of Bonhoeffer to Maria and of Bethge to Bonhoeffer's niece, the Gestapo arrested Hans von Dohnanyi, Bonhoeffer's uncle and a conspirator against Hitler, and, only a day later, they took Bonhoeffer, on whom the enforcers had gained plenty of incriminating evidence. Through several of the first months Bonhoeffer and Bethge exchanged letters that are not part of *Letters and Papers from Prison* and therefore are not part of this biography of the book. The first preserved letter to Bethge is dated November 18, six months after the imprisonment began. It included not only the comment on *tristitia* but also, more happily, reflection on Bethge's marriage. Bonhoeffer followed this with one on Christmas Eve in which he thanked God that his niece Renate would be there to "stand by" Eberhard. A softer familial touch appeared: he had to instruct Renate no longer to call him "Uncle."[5]

The topics of the letters seem to be generated at random and some make up a grab bag of informative data. Bonhoeffer discussed how he had wished to be present at the Bethge wedding and that he had later also hoped to be able to baptize the couple's first child. Meanwhile, he announced, he was undertaking a bold enterprise. He was to spend prison time writing a novel, which he subsequently did. And he reported on his reading more than twice through the Old Testament while, in order to relax his mind, devouring the books of the middle-level German novelist Adalbert Stifter, whose writings somehow spoke to him in the prison years. At the end, reflecting a shadow that had to be part of prison existence, we read a plea for and a pledge of friendship with the man who would produce this book. "And if it should be determined that we never see each other again, then let us think of each other to the end with gratitude and forgiveness, and may God grant to us then that we one day stand praying for each other and praising and giving thanks with each other before God's throne."[6]

Coloring expressions in the letters are varieties of displays of emotion. As confined people will do, in this opening sequence of letters he praised his fiancée and voiced a longing for her and their eventual marriage. Just as quickly he had to turn, to mourn the deaths in action on the eastern front of students with whom he had shared life at the clandestine "preacher seminary" at remote Finkenwalde. On that front, these former students gave their lives for a cause in which they could not believe or at least that they could not understand. In later letters Bonhoeffer, having heard of the death of one or the other of these, would mourn and inquire for details about memorials. Little news of action on that eastern front where they died could reach Bonhoeffer, who was not allowed access to newspapers or radio.

During the months in which the early letters were written, while Bethge still was able to perform tasks for the Gossner Mission during his assignments in Switzerland and Germany, the threats to Bonhoeffer's future kept growing. First he merely awaited trial. Readers of the book receive little detail about what this involved, since it was too dangerous for him to write explicitly about any of it. Instead, the letters from this period repeatedly celebrated the friendship of these two writers, along with mentions of friends and family in general. While the letters show Bonhoeffer hoping for an early trial and, against all hope, one must say, picturing eventual freedom, a dark future loomed much of the time, as was evident in the letters.

A New World to Enter

Despite the threat to his future as a conspirator against Hitler, Bonhoeffer continued to ponder marriage, a subject he did not handle well. He envisioned and dreamed of a postwar visit to Italy by the two Bethges and the future couple, Dietrich and Maria. But he lost credibility among some readers when, in one of his letters, he suggested that the two men should complete such a trip by going on to Israel without wife and bride.[7] It also does not take an agitated feminist to read Bonhoeffer as a patriarchal sort in the wedding sermon he wrote from prison in May 1943. It was mainly a several page homily on wifely submission.[8] In any case, thoughts of honeymoons and future friendship were deferred when it was learned that Bethge could no longer evade the call to service. The published letters suggest something of his world. From July 1943 until early 1944 he was in training in Poland. Then he was sent to the scene of military action in Italy.

The purchaser and reader of Bethge's achievement in the form of *Letters and Papers from Prison* did not have to read more than the first couple of pages in order to enter a world that is at the same time beckoning and forbidding. The first letter speaks of a birthday party, a blanket and vest, dry bread, cigarettes, and then, abruptly, of "the considerable internal adjustment demanded by . . . an unexpected arrest and having to come to terms and put up with a completely new situation" that led him to a mix of emotions, including enrichment and possible torment.[9]

If the genre and tone of *Letters and Papers from Prison* were different from most books of the time sold as theology, the character of personal faith was almost immediately apparent. The author and his correspondents went back to basics, as one learns while reading the fifth letter included in the collection. It was from Hans von Dohnanyi, the prisoner's brother-in-law, who was arrested when Bonhoeffer had been and was to be executed on the same day as Bonhoeffer was, April 9, 1945. "I now read the Bible a lot; it is the only book that prevents my thoughts from drifting off all the time."[10]

Those readers who are moved by the agonized, yearning, but also often celebratory tone of the correspondence can better understand all this when they learn that during the months of imprisonment editor but then still soldier Bethge, on leave on November 26, 1943, was allowed to see Bonhoeffer. Even Maria was permitted to visit, but the engaged couple were not permitted to be alone together and certainly were not supposed to touch. On one of the very rare visits she impulsively did lunge toward and embrace her fiancé. One suspects that this breach of prison conduct occurred because some guards were at least slightly sympathetic—and Maria's family, the Wedemeyers, were privileged and had enough connections to make possible the occasional slight relaxing of prison rules.

I have not made much mention of additional items that Bethge bound with the letters; writings that became the "papers" of "Letters and Papers." The last one among them, a piece that was of help to scholars as it had been to Bethge, was "An Outline for a Book." One could tell from it and from what Bonhoeffer wrote about it that the curtain was closing on the life of Bonhoeffer. Bethge wrote a final letter September 30, 1944, as concerns for security had to take precedence over everything else. The end was still months off, but from Bonhoeffer there could only be silence. We have no more letters or papers or outlines.

The Life of a Book

In the next chapter I will tell the story of how the book came to be, largely because of the work of its author's friend, Bethge. Here, instead, we pick up the finished product and see it launched. *Letters and Papers from Prison*, like other books, has a life. This one, begotten in Germany at midcentury, has traveled to all continents and spoken to readers through almost twenty languages. One student, years later, reported finding a new Spanish copy of it, *Resistencia y sumisón,* in Buchholtz's grand bookstore in Bogota, Colombia. Such a find was replicated thousands of times around the world. Through the years other students and friends who knew of my interest in the author alerted me and others to their discovery of works like *Yu Zhong shu jian* in Japan along with other translations purchasable in Korea, Taiwan, as well as many points in the West. Not many German works with topics like this one make their way into Serbo-Croatian, but a Zagreb publisher in 1974 offered it as *Otpor I predanje,* while Czech, Polish, Finnish, and other publishing companies also found a market and a readership for it.

The shortened version of the German original title was *Widerstand und Ergebung,* meaning "Resistance and Submission." That unrevealing and not very beckoning title needs and will receive comment later. The book in its infancy, as we learn from early responses to the collection, was not favorably greeted everywhere. Old-school and academically straight-laced theologians for the most part considered the whole project to be something almost subversive and scorned it. The first American edition and the source of my own original encounter with the book, in 1954, did not serve the letters well, for it was unfortunately titled *Prisoner for God*.[11] Its publisher later and more appropriately scuttled that name and soon substituted for it *Letters and Papers from Prison*, and so it has been known in English ever since. Given such titles, this mysterious stranger among theology books, reposed at home on bookshelves in many cultures, will not have revealed much about itself to those who accidentally have come upon it. The German title could suggest in the minds of new readers the theme of resistance and submission but gave no clues to the context of the experience that needed resistance or demanded submission. Such a title could connote, for instance, anything from reaction to arrests by police, to sexual encounters, to full-scale war.

"Letters" by many notables abound simply as collections in books, and from them historians and voyeurs draw most of their knowledge about people long dead. "Papers" can include birth and death certificates along with manuscripts and other rich sources for biographers. That word, nondescript in essence, by itself points nowhere and gives no indication as to why

Polish or Swedish readerships should be attracted to the book or could know what they were getting if they bought it or checked it out of the library. The first word in the title that might tantalize and attract readers is "Prison."

Prison letters, with their own honored place in history, and books collecting them make up a genre that can be counted on as being revealing and even alluring among biographers, prison reformers, psychologists, trial lawyers, and sympathetic citizens, depending upon the cause and character of particular imprisonments. One can picture a reader in this varied company who, while making a regular stop to scan used books in junk bins at stores from Berkeley to Boston or from Cape Town to London, eyes a well-worn and tattered dust jacket wrapped around a book that some graduate student has overused or thinks she has outgrown. This browser soon becomes another buyer, and this *Letters and Papers from Prison* has found a new home. That evening the owner, we imagine, takes time to examine his loot from the day and moves emotionally a bit closer to the life of his purchase. He considers the author's name, Dietrich Bonhoeffer, which is German, but Germans live not only in Germany, so that name by itself offers few clues to the contents and suggests to him nothing exotic.

Odds are that the reader has picked up the edition read by most English-speakers through the years, Dietrich Bonhoeffer, *Letters and Papers from Prison: New Greatly Enlarged Edition*, published by Macmillan in

New York in 1978. It included so much more material than had the original that its translator, British biblical scholar Reginald Fuller, later joined by other translators and editors, would certainly have advised the owners of the old *Prisoner for God* to send it to the book recyclers. Editions followed editions, culminating in the German volume of 1998 and in English translation in 2010—the edition on which I draw.

To speak, as I have just done, of how "editions followed editions" is to overpass crucial elements in the life of almost any book but certainly does an injustice to the part these successive editions have played in the life of *Letters and Papers from Prison*. While publishers adorn new products with fresh dust jackets, the changes represent far more than what a change of clothes means for a biographical subject. Year after year since 1951 new materials kept being unearthed, while fresh insights offered by conference-goers and long-needed reference materials came to be available. The version which, whether adorned with a jacket or being bare in paperback form, is destined to dominate research for years to come is the 1998 (German) and 2010 (English) publication.

The fact that the title page lists twelve translators and editors is one indication of what it takes to do justice to what was born on manuscript pages in the Tegel prison cell. Most responsible for this contribution to the seventeen-volume and certainly definitive work in English, building on the German original, are the International Bonhoeffer Society, the general editor Victoria J. Barnett, and John de Gruchy, editor of the English edition.

Books, like authors, live and eventually die. To their publishers and writers, this dying is represented by a book going out of print, as some do in their infancy, within months. Others survive until over-crowded libraries deaccession and pulp them to make room for fresh publications. Today many books are likely to experience a second life on the Internet, in cyberspace. Books as we have known them also "die on the vine," say booksellers when they cannot move them. Their vital life is gone when agents cannot inter-est media to nurture their reputations with publicity. They linger and then expire when reviewers pass them by and then pass them off to used-book shops that bury them in recycling bins. Some, alas, are stillborn and never attract sales and notice. Think of them as reposing in paupers' graves. R.I.P.

More happily, chroniclers speak of the career of a living book just as they write of authors. Conception occurs in the mind of a writer who brings it to birth, after which it attracts attention, gets read, exerts influ-ence, and may enter the canon of a particular culture. Most will simply suffer neglect and meet with indiffer-ence. On occasion someone will rediscover a book and put out a new edition, having made the argument that "there is still life" in the book or that "it deserves to be resurrected." Historians and historically informed lit-erary critics subsequently assess and locate the book, and in so doing they enhance and extend its life.

While we can have no death date for Bonhoeffer's book, nor would we want one, we can trace its birth. The last letter in this book of *Letters and Papers from Prison* was written as a Christmas greeting in 1944, twenty weeks before the Second World War ended in Europe. That end came twenty-nine days after its author had been executed by the Nazis for his role in the resistance to Hitler and an aborted attempt to assassinate him. Were it not for the fact that the author's best friend had saved the letters from and to the conspirator's family, fiancée, and this friend himself, there would never have been the book. Without wanting to stretch the metaphor too far, it is proper to say that without Bethge the book would never have been conceived, or that it would have been aborted.

Instead, the book took on the proverbial life of its own and, given the attention it receives in the new millennium, we can say that it thrives in midcareer. Most letters by German religious scholars and others who attracted any public interest at all did not survive the bombings, fires, chaos, and neglect that were part of the war and so are lost. There are welcome exceptions, but most letters that were saved and have since been found did not receive the custodial care and editing that friend Bethge gave to these. Those few that did find a new home have seldom received the world-wide attention given this one and may be thought of as dead letters. *Letters and Papers from Prison,* however, ages well and deserves that "life of . . ." just as notable humans deserve biographies.

Reincarnations

On those grounds and with such understandings, this work appears in the Princeton University Press series, "Lives of Great Religious Books." To speak of the treatment of a never-animate subject as a biography is to court mishaps and misfortune. A biography is a "bio-," a life, picking up on the beginning of the word in the Greek-rooted *bios.* The root indicates something animate, for example, as human. To talk about writing or reading a biography of a book is to rely on analogy and metaphor, both of which can be extended to the absurd point that they distract rather than inform. These literary forms can busy the reader with the task of observing the performance of the author rather than engaging the career of the book. In analogy, there is a difference within every element of sameness and some kind of sameness in every difference. When analogy can carry the story forward and help make it memorable, it will be put to service here. When it does not or might not, I shall, untroubled, suppress it and not trouble the reader with comparisons and metaphors.

We are picturing the physical object, *Letters and Papers from Prison,* as the book picked up almost randomly by someone who has an interest in prison literature and the Hitler years in Germany, but not necessarily in the philosophy of existence or theology. A dust jacket would certainly have identified the main author as a theologian, but this turns out to have been a theologian of a different sort, one who did not

match the stereotypes—and there *are* stereotypes!—
or at least one who underwent circumstances that dif-
fered vastly from the usual. Many books by professors
like Bonhoeffer and scholarly pastors like Bethge
would be well-researched, learned, formidable, perhaps turgid, full of allusions to authors and subjects
that hold interest only for other theologians. Such a
book would include footnotes so long and complex
that they would have bred their own footnotes. That is
the conventional picture, though one could point to
many twentieth-century exceptions, even in theology,
such as a commentary on *The Epistle to the Romans*
by Swiss theologian Karl Barth, which served as a
wake-up call immediately after the First World War.[12]
(Barth far exceeded all other theologians as an influence on Bonhoeffer.) Their authors became public
figures whose existential mold and personal experience helped break the ordinary scholastic and academic patterns.

Letters and Papers from Prison presents itself as a
manufactured object, a book like other books, whose
career can be marked and measured as such. This one,
in its English-language versions alone, has through the
decades been reincarnated, clothed in various dust
jackets, bindings, and fonts, each of which will provide hints about the provenances and milieus of its
travels. Those of us who love books pay much attention to all these. Thus my own most cherished German copy is a chaste black-bound book published in
Munich in 1955. Most tattered in the collection are

two copies "Printed in Great Britain" on brittle paper that has now turned yellow-brown and may before long turn to dust. This sorry condition resulted from their exposure to elements that beset them at summer retreats and conferences or on flights where their pocket size commended itself. I retain visual images, as readers of favored books do, of where—meaning on which part of a page—this or that memorable quotation appears. Similarly, one recalls perceptions and memories of friends known through the years.

If we would speak of the physical object as the body of a book, a biography of a book will specially focus on its soul, the content and message it emits, and then the human responses to it. Such a biography is its own kind of narrative and analysis. It treats book reviews as events and is therefore not to be conceived of as an overlong book review or a collection of reviews. It will, of course, draw on some of them, because they help serve as dialogue-partners with a variety of readers during the life of a book and for historical recall after its decline. A biography of a book is also not in any essential way a work of literary or theological criticism, though critics cited here do make their contribution to this life At root, biographies are stories. This, then, is the story of *Letters and Papers from Prison* by Dietrich Bonhoeffer. Though, of course, the author had a life of *his* own, in the form of experiences that reach far beyond the margins and covers in this book, it is his letters that give life to the biography and merit notice in new generations.

To this point we have conjured up a reader who came across the book and took it home because she was at least mildly interested in prison literature. We further picture that, if she is patient after opening her purchase and the book is compelling, she finds it speaking to her out of a world unfamiliar to her. After the fifth line of the 1978 edition she finds the editor speaking of "theological meditations" along with "personal relationships," both of which, she quickly learns, relate to the author's confinement in a Nazi prison during World War II. What will soon become clear is that many references in the book may not quicken curiosity or at first glance have much prospect of luring her to these interests.

As an experiment, one might sample the "L's" in the bibliography and ask whoever in the mainstream culture ever heard of people named Lapide, Latmiral, Leber, Lehmann, Leibholtz, Lilje, Lübeck, Lukens (whom we now know from the title page). In that catalog, I skipped only Leibniz and Luther, whose names will be familiar. The subject index in the 1978 version is even more forbidding. It begins "*Abwehr, Accidie,* Act, Accustomed, Acquiescence"—words that are not promising candidates for the A-lists of any but a few specialists. If our purchaser of that book persists in reading, she—and let's also imagine "he"—will soon find a context for such words. So it is with subjects in the biographies of most people with whom we have not previously been on intimate terms. The letter-writer Bonhoeffer and the editors of his papers do place them in context and briefly identify each in footnotes, so the going is easy.

By now it should be clear that the issue of genre is here a topic about which I am concerned, for the reader's protection as well as my own. These letters come from their author's final two years and cannot begin to represent a balanced story of his whole life, even when references to them occasion some footnotes or explain themselves in the course of the page. Similarly, stress on the biography of the book, not the author, protects me from suggesting with hubris that I could improve on or supplement the great biography by Bethge. The eleven-hundred-page English version of that book is only a sample of the Bonhoeffer bibliography, which runs into thousands of items in many languages. With such a background and context, the only way to discipline me as its author and to force some constraints has been to limit, as much as possible, comment on other books written earlier by Bonhoeffer. Incidents and writings from outside those temporal boundaries will receive explanation if they must be mentioned as they throw particular lights on what is in the book whose biography this is.

For a quick illustration, I point to the fact that Bonhoeffer had a twin sister, Sabine, who was very important to him and who appears on twenty pages of Bethge's biography. She would go unmentioned here, had the writer of the letters not referred to her five times and had she not been married to a Jew, a lawyer, with whom she took refuge in England. Since the reception of *Letters and Papers from Prison* in Great Britain and among Jews is at least a small part of the biography of the book, it is the two or three allusions or slight references to her in the letters from her imprisoned brother that would draw notice. Informed commentators assume that the references were slight because her letter-writing twin needed to protect her from unwanted notice. Friends from his years before 1943 will go unmentioned here unless his letters refer to them, in which case they become part of the biography of this book.

Having evoked a scene in which this book falls almost accidentally into the hands of a browser, it is time to grow purposeful and to take the risk that goes with making the claim that it merits attention among a very diverse public, two-thirds of a century and more after the letters and papers within it were written. Many volumes of prison letters are available; so why read *this* collection? Library shelves are full of books on resistance to Hitler, while on other book stacks there are works by many theologians of the twentieth century. Why, by taking up the reading of this book, add to a new generation of respondents in its biographical train? Without playing games about calling a book the "greatest" this or that and then listing it along with other candidates for such laud, I will venture to call it what so many in its history have called it, a classic.

Conversing with a Modern Classic

The reader will better understand that claim and more helpfully connect it to this twentieth-century book, one that in the eyes of many may not seem aged enough to be a classic, if I say something about what a classic is and what it can do in company with the activity of the reader. Such a discussion can also help illumine aspects of the book. This one is so full of bizarre turns, apparent betrayals, and incongruities that a reader may ask and seek answers: What is a theological professor doing when taking part in a conspiracy to kill a dictator, practicing deception, lying, breaking the law, and wasting readers' time with apparently trivial matters such as requests for toiletries or passing on gossip? Call a book about all that a classic? Also, in many respects it does not provide a mode or a template for the living of ordinary lives. Mentioning its relative youth, as I have done, may lead the questioning reader to wonder at the use of the term "classic" about a book that is so young. Augustine's *Confessions* and Dante's *Divine Comedy* as classics have weathered the tests of readers for centuries. Now, it is fair to ask, is the reference to classic in relation to the Bonhoeffer book anything more than hyperbole from the author's devotees or comments in blurbs, designed to boost sales and circulation?

What in the life of a book has to happen to it or what does it achieve through its readers in order to deserve the "classic" label? Catholic theologian David

Tracy fussed with that term at considerable length and with subtlety in his *Plurality and Ambiguity: Hermeneutics, Religion, Hope,* and I wrestled with his wrestling with the term as on occasion we cotaught graduate students. "On historical grounds," Tracy wrote, "classics are simply those texts that have helped found or form a particular culture." Also, he added, "on more explicitly hermeneutical grounds, classics are those texts that bear an excess and permanence of meaning, yet always resist definitive interpretation." Paradoxically, classic texts, born in particularity, "have the possibility of being universal in their effect."[13] In that case, calling this book a classic, as many do, is a bid to the reader to engage the Bonhoeffer text in a particular way. Tracy and other students of what is classical bid that reader to test such a book by conversing with it.

Accustomed as moderns are to thinking of conversation as oral exchange among humans, they may find it awkward or contrived to carry its meaning over to the medium of print. But to conceive of a book as having a life of its own and thus as warranting a biography opens the possibility that the reader will be engaged with that life, as in oral conversation. The conversational mode is easier to adopt with the unfinished-appearing and, indeed, truly unfinished set of letters and papers than it is with books that are apparently seamless, closed, and finished products. Bonhoeffer's letters are full of invitations, questions, and expectations, some of them met and followed up on in his own short personal life and most of them not. The author lives on in this book, and the reader converses. Here is Tracy: "We converse with one another. We can also converse with texts. If we read well, then we are conversing with the text. No human being is simply a passive recipient of texts. We inquire. We question. We converse. Just as there is no purely autonomous text, so too there is no purely passive reader. There is only that interaction named conversation."[14]

Before that summary paragraph Tracy offered advice that, if followed, will be of aid to the reader when Bonhoeffer in his letters and papers confronts him or her with difficult, sometimes unclear, often paradoxical themes. Such counsel will come in handy when the reader enters the debates and conversations over the author's most controversial and chancy discourse concerning faith and life, for instance in what he will call a "world that has come of age." Variations on this and other admittedly problematic themes become a major part of the aftermath to the publication that a lone reader in her library or a class will confront. The book, the author, and the reader meet:

> Conversation is a game with some hard rules: say only what you mean; say it as accurately as you can; listen to and respect what the other says, however different or other; be willing to correct or defend your opinions if challenged by the conversation partner; be willing to argue if necessary, to confront if demanded, to endure necessary conflict, to change your mind if the evidence suggests it.

These are merely some generic rules for questioning. As good rules, they are worth keeping in mind in case the questioning does begin to break down. In a sense they are merely variations of the transcendental imperative elegantly articulated by Bernard Lonergan: "Be attentive, be intelligent, be responsible, be loving, and, if necessary, change."[15]

When peers meet and talk with each other, or when a generous mentor and an assertive student engage each other, something goes on that has the chance of altering worldviews. So it can be with the Bonhoeffer book. Every time I read Augustine's *Confessions*, I come away looking at myself and the world in a different way. My friend the late Jaroslav Pelikan said that annually he reread *The Divine Comedy* in the original. He cannot each time have learned many new things about the poem he had read so often. He did it in the spirit of its author, in words that Goethe voiced in *Faust*: "What you have as heritage, Take now as task; For thus you will make it your own!" He was each time reckoning with a tradition and, in a way, becoming part of it. Similarly, many readers all over the world have testified to the changes they experienced after having "conversed" with Bonhoeffer's letters and papers.

The conversation with a classic also offers readers a chance to hold up the mirror to themselves. For example, the reader of *The Brothers Karamazov* does not in it seek a road map of Russia or information about the land. He stands the potential of learning more about himself and his world through the reading and conversation. In this case the biography of a book can serve where face-to-face encounters are not possible. On Bonhoeffer's pages one does not learn how to conspire against the life of a dictator or how to survive in prison, but one might learn more about the world in which one lives today. In the case of this posthumous work the author cannot be available as a living person, but he writes his letters and papers in such a way that revelations and "aha!" moments can occur.

Letters and Papers from Prison is highly personal, including raw material that might have been in use had Bonhoeffer written a memoir. As it turns out, it is as if he and his compiling editor Bethge had heard the advice by American publisher William Sloan, who told writers of autobiographical pieces that the reader is not saying of any such book something like: "Tell me about you." Instead it is, "Tell me about me; as I use your book and life as a mirror." The details of the life of a reader in a cozy study or a library will not begin to match those of Bonhoeffer, but this book, which has its own life, can serve the reader, who brings her own life to the reading, to experience change. Were it a "how-to" book, the reader could take lessons, close it, and live and think as before, simply making use of forgettable technical directions. *Letters and Papers from Prison* opens a conversation and, with it, a different world.

In a liberal arts curriculum, *Letters and Papers from Prison* would be classified among the humanities, and now I as its biographer invite readers to think of it as a contribution in that genre, one that can offer a changed view of existence. As the introduction to a report on *The Humanities in American Life* suggests, "through the humanities we reflect on the fundamental question: what does it mean to be human? The humanities offer clues but never a complete answer." They have their limits, "but by awakening a sense of what it might be like to be someone else or to live in another time or culture, they tell us about ourselves, stretch our imagination, and enrich our experience. They increase our distinctively human potential."[16] Many readers report that some such enrichment and increase happened to them when they read *Letters and Papers from Prison*. One hopes that a biography of this book will lead to further "awakenings."

Biographers know how to outline books on human lives. The familiar stops along the way typically include references to ancestry, birth, the stages of life, marriages or not, achievements, perceptions by others, accidents, and death. Biographers of books will appeal to certain readerships, for example, bibliophiles, by discussing the bindings, the papers used, the fonts, the editions, and sales. Here there will be casual references to a few of them, but our humanistic (in the sense of the "humanities" as just referenced) interests call for different accents Some analogies between lives and books work well, as when one writes about the antecedents, conception, birth, and some of the passages of the lives of books like Bonhoeffer's. Equally to the point here will be reference to the reception of the book, its travels to various cultures, and its relation to major events of the time.

To keep the book within the boundaries set for this series, I shall concentrate on materials—"secondary sources," in academic lingo—that manifest a certain landmark quality because they appeared as books or as substantial chapters in books. Wandering into the vastness of periodical literature, news stories, or the Internet would be illuminating, but the temptation to do so has to be resisted. Bibliographers note that there are hundreds of thousands of references to the life and works of Bonhoeffer, many of them concentrating on this one book.[17] This biography of a book is about books that served as conversation partners to author Bonhoeffer and editor Bethge, in a conversation that is now being taken up by a new generation of readers.

Dietrich Bonhoeffer
in a prison yard

Bonhoeffer, second from
the right, with Italian Air
Force prisoners of war,
with a Sergeant Napp,
who had the picture taken

Window in Bonhoeffer's cell at Tegel

Berlin-Tegel prison, Bonhoeffer's cell
marked by a penciled "x"

Prisoners' quarters at Flössenbürg Concentration Camp

Execution site at Flössenbürg

Wedding of Eberhard Bethge
and Renate Schleicher

Fiancee Maria
von Wedemeyer,
taken in 1942

The "Gradual" Editor

CHAPTER 2

The reader of letters and papers that issue from the unpromising circumstances with which we are becoming familiar cannot fail to be curious about how the letters morphed into a book. Eberhard Bethge, who brought the book to life, devoted only the first pages of a preface to an enlarged edition in 1970 to detail the process. He told how in 1950–51 he had wanted to make available for a few friends some short, "specifically theological, meditations" from Tegel. Even before the war was over he transcribed a few extracts to circulate to these friends during a time when he was still desiring to guard the privacy of the people around Bonhoeffer. We read on the first page of the existence of his very young fiancée and of letters exchanged between the couple that were published after her death. For the rest, twenty years after the first extracts had been printed, the publisher commissioned a complete revision, since the book was already then being considered a classic. Bethge in 1970 alerted readers, writing that many things they would have liked to have known never appeared. This was the case because of the activity of censors and Bonhoeffer's own desire to protect the identity of his coconspirators and other friends and relatives. Despite the tardy appearance of the letters and papers and the natural limits to the enterprise, the editor said he was confident that readers would welcome learning from what he did publish how Bonhoeffer's theology had been "interwoven with the course of his life."[1]

Bethge was often called upon to tell more of the history of the book than he had chosen to include within its covers. Thus he described it well for an American audience and readership during a year he spent at Harvard in 1957–58.[2] In the years soon after the Second World War, as he put it, he only gradually became convinced that these fragmentary works should be published, and, though inexperienced as an editor, he felt called to put the book together. He looked back: six months after the Gestapo arrested Bonhoeffer on April 5, 1943, letters started to come from Tegel to Bonhoeffer's fiancée, his parents, and Bethge, who was also permitted twice to visit Bonhoeffer in prison. "When I myself was finally arrested, in October, 1944, I had time only to draw his last letters quickly from my pockets and destroy them." Some of those that Bethge had gathered and preserved from Bonhoeffer's desk were the nucleus of the consequent book.

Bethge had taken on the major task of editing other scraps Bonhoeffer had left into a version of what was to have been Bonhoeffer's life work, a book on ethics. When that work appeared, Bethge wrote, he had "waited anxiously for the echo. The echo when it came was scarcely audible." Ironically, it was instead the later publication of the letters, including in their English form, *Prisoner for God*, that won readers for the presumably more important *Ethics*.

To produce the book of letters and papers, Bethge had to resurrect their texts from their hiding places, even from tin cans, buried in a garden by "the women." Bethge added in parentheses: "A few of my letters still show distinct marks of the damp mold that had begun to cause the paper to disintegrate." Others came to light because a prison guard, Corporal Knobloch, who was loyal to Bonhoeffer, had risked his own life by forwarding secret mail. Bonhoeffer's mother had hidden those she received in her gas mask canister buried behind her small garden house in a Berlin suburb. Much that was stored in such places was lost. Bethge regretted such loss but, undeterred, made a virtue of necessity as he pointed to the genre of the book that appeared seven years after the material in it had been written. Emphatically, he reminded readers, this was not a theological essay on radical themes but "genuine letters . . . tinged as they are with all the emotions, sometimes more and sometimes less rigorously controlled, of a man in a prison cell."

The editor appended one note of high drama filled with pathos. The final letters, which Bonhoeffer wrote after he began describing to his friend some controversial theological probes that were to appear near the end of the book, Bethge confessed, might have thrown light on those that survived and that tantalized or perplexed later scholars:

> But these September letters [1944] were the ones I had burned in the fireplace just before my own arrest. At the time I had a feeling of relief at the thought that they could no longer incriminate or bring misfortune on anyone. (No member of the Gestapo ever learned of the extensive and illegal correspondence carried on during the years 1943 and 1944.) . . . Today I am afflicted with the tormenting afterthought that I was responsible for the destruction of what may have contained decisive developments of Bonhoeffer's ideas, but developments which I can no longer recall. There is no longer anything from Bonhoeffer, then . . . .

When he was arrested in October 1944, he remembered, he had time only to draw the last letters quickly from his pockets and destroy them. The life of this book began in peril.

Letters and Papers from Prison is in many ways an accidental book. Once when asked about the origin of the book he edited and published, Bethge declared that the volume had not sprung into his mind as a quick inspiration. The word "gradual" was a constant in his story. He mentioned that at one time he had thought the imprisoned Bonhoeffer would "be successful," which meant, in part, that he would survive the war. "And even when this proved not to be the case," Bethge explained,

> it was only gradually that I became convinced that the fragments of his writings ought to be preserved and made available, and even more gradually that perhaps the contexts and relationships of these fragmentary works deserved also to be recorded. The task of becoming an editor and publisher of posthumous documents was thrust upon me without any previous experience in the techniques and requirements of such a responsibility to history. I belonged to the theological generation in Germany in the thirties that thought of engagement in pure science as a cowardly evasion of duties on the battle line. As a matter of fact, German theology in those years suffered seriously from the lack of men well-trained in theological research.[3]

The Bonhoeffer materials carried or smuggled out of Tegel prison came gradually to Bethge, and, as he confessed, the idea of this book also grew gradually. The gender of the metaphor is inapt, but the function of the editor is well summed up in the word "midwifery." Bethge served as midwife, enabling the book to come into being, in this case out of the letters, scraps of paper, outlines, proposals, and anything else that came his way directly from friend Dietrich, his relatives and friends, and, on some occasions, in the form of official documents. These scattered and sometimes apparently random leavings would not have matured into a book, which then came to have a life of its own, without Bethge's complex and patient work. He was too modest to put his name on his book's title page. We can be less modest and quite honest in figuratively putting him there and devoting a chapter to what he was about as he gathered and edited the letters and papers until they became the book originally published as *Widerstand und Ergebung.*

The birth of a book in any humanistic discipline in Germany typically occurred in a monastic cell, a library carrel, a university study, an aerie, or an attic atop a Promethean professor's abode. In those cases, after years of confinement in the academy, preferably in seminar rooms that serve as clinics, an author, along with earnest young associates in residence and with a name heavily doctored with initials like D. Phil., Lic., and so forth, produced a manuscript. The utilized archives had been stuffed with handwritten manuscripts from earlier centuries, but during much of the twentieth century, a typical pipe-smoking author would wield a typewriter and turn out draft pages. Alternatively, important and self-important at once, and depending upon his status, he may have dictated the whole book to a bored but long-suffering secretary. Such a professor might try out parts of chapters on doctoral candidates, who would help refine its points or propose additional areas of research. After all such processes, still necessarily to be followed by proofreading, a published version of the book would be born. It would be picked apart by the author's rivals, lavishly endorsed by friends and acolytes, and savaged by reviewers whose comments might run almost as long as the book itself. Finis.

Fostering the Book: Eberhard Bethge's Role

Of course, that composite is a caricature, though it is not difficult to find many instances of each imagined detail. My purpose in going on a bit about the stereotypical process was to set up the contrast to what happened when, after the war, Bethge had to make a decision. He pondered what to do with those letters and papers that had fallen into his custody during and after their production between 1942 and 1945. Bethge, be it noted, was himself a Wittenberg University–trained theologian, whose follow-up education to prepare him for preaching and pastoral ministry occurred in extraordinary circumstances, mainly in the clandestine school for ministers led by Bonhoeffer late in the 1930s. This was at an illegal seminary named Finkenwalde, chiefly in farm buildings in the north of Germany, now Zdroje in Poland. He was later well-seasoned in life experiences as a reluctant draftee in the German army, and after the war he further ripened as a pastor and editor.

Back at the illegal Finkenwalde seminary he had bonded so strongly with teacher Bonhoeffer that some of the dozens of fellow students resented his access to

their tutor. Their bond resembled a "particular friendship," which is the rather technical term used by Catholics when they warn seminarians or sisters in con-
vents against the potential for cloying intimacy among
the few at the expense of general fellowship among
the many. But a warm spirit of fellowship and experience of common life among the students characterized their time in the school. Not all went smoothly.
Bethge and the rest of the seminarians later recalled
the intrusion of a truly disruptive element in that seminary life, which had occurred when, in the course of
their studies, teacher Bonhoeffer planted calls for resistance to the Nazi regime among them. Not all of
them were prepared for any call that might unsettle
such would-be pastors as they were on the point of
launching careers.

When that seminary in the farm country was broken up and closed by authorities and when the war
came, both men did what they could to continue
theological work. The school had itself been too small
and remote an instrument to serve as a center of resistance to Nazism's takeover of the church and the
havoc it was causing in the world. The chief Christian
instrument for opposition, mentioned eight times in
the Bonhoeffer letters and assumed throughout them,
was what came to be called the Confessing Church.
This force was led by a minority band of ministers and
congregational leaders, mainly Lutheran but also Reformed, who challenged the official German church,
most of which was passively or actively lining up with

the oppressive and presumptuous government. They were, in turn, rendered suspect in the eyes of nondissenters, who disdained and often hounded them for not being friendly enough or at least insufficiently acquiescent to the Nazi regime.

Through the early war years Bonhoeffer was working on his major book *Ethics*, but he also kept being called into action to test the ethics or lack of such in church, seminary, and nation. During that prewar period the noose that would carry "traitor" Bonhoeffer to death was figuratively being fashioned, though several years of imprisonment while the writing of letters and papers went on kept the rope from being used until on April 9, 1945, during the last month of the European war. Bethge, always opposed to Nazism, had evaded the military draft as long as he could while he developed relations with exiles or friends of other dissenters. Many of these were named in the letters. Some took refuge in neutral Switzerland, which Bonhoeffer also visited before his own imprisonment.

It is not too dramatic to say that had Bethge not done his storing and editing work, the only Bonhoeffer the larger world would know was the promising theologian whose career had been cut short by the war. A biography of *Letters and Papers from Prison* could properly begin with a note: "Born, 1950, in Eberhard Bethge's study." There, as we learned, five years after the war, sensing or becoming convinced that he owed to a larger world the letters and papers of which he was now custodian, Bethge edited and published a selection. He had some reason to be uneasy as he published the first edition. For instance, he was disseminating words by a theologian who was not everyone's hero. Among those who picked up the tangled skeins of theology in the half dozen years after the war in Germany were some who thought of Bonhoeffer as a conspirator against Hitler and thus against the government, as well as a theological experimenter who spoke critically of many Christian practices, though from within the church. The weary routine-loving pastors among them wanted to resume normal practices, and a book like this fresh one could only upset them. We learn from early responses to the first published collection that many theologians scorned the whole project of this book as something almost subversive.

Editor Bethge, who was always alert to matters dialectical, had to name the book. He seized on the two words that Bonhoeffer had used in a letter dated February 21, 1944: *Widerstand und Ergebung*, "resistance" and "submission." The second noun of that title represented one side of that dialectic with which even the mildest protestor covered his traces by making some submissive compromises. Readers can discern in the two words an implied interplay of forces, revelations, and concealments. Bonhoeffer had been hoping to learn more about his fate but noted to Bethge "with amazement that in fact nothing has happened for six months." Then he confessed, "I have often wondered here where we are to draw the line between necessary *resistance* to 'fate,' and equally necessary *submission*."[4]

Since Bethge outlived Bonhoeffer by a half century and was able to contribute to the life and health of the book in its later career, whether by lecturing, participating in conferences, or further publishing, his role in shaping the book remained more than that of a mere editor—if any editors should think of their work as "mere." And Bethge had at hand plenty of rich material on both the "resistance" and "submission" themes, as his own life story demonstrates. We lack elaborations on many aspects of Bonhoeffer's private life. Much that he did write about has been lost. Not all the letters that Bonhoeffer wrote and sent ever reached their destinations, not all were saved, and no one could know how many writings, if developed, might make up what would have been a mature corpus.

In the life of a book, there comes a time when its author begins to picture an audience, a readership. At the end of the collection of letters, indeed, in the last surviving message from prison, we find Bonhoeffer writing about the saved letters and papers: "You can imagine how pleased I am that you're bothering about them. How indispensable I would now find a matter-of-fact talk to clarify this whole problem. When that comes about, it will be one of the great days of my life."[5]

More fortunately for serious scholars, on August 23, 1944, referring to a chapter on what came to be called "A Stocktaking of Christianity," Bonhoeffer did a bit of self-editing and declared that what he had thought and written was "too clumsy," so it "can't be printed yet."

In such lines he sounded like a conscientious if conventional author awaiting a good copy editor, or like someone who was planning to put his writing in shape on his own. In any case, the noun he used describes part of the book-creating process very well. He concluded: "It will have to go through the 'treatment facility'" later on. His editors note that this was an affectionate way of speaking about his long conversations with Bethge.[6] Bethge did serve in the "treatment facility" role and produced the book.

An Uncertain Birth and Reception

Bethge was guarded about the first publication, sometimes unsure about whether such private correspondence should have gone public at all. Like many a diarist and letter-writer, Bonhoeffer was sufficiently mindful of the potential fate of prison writings such as his to lead him to keep one eye on an eventual public. It was this mix of letters that were to be dug up one day in the garden of his fiancée Maria von Wedemeyer's family, among other places where they had been hidden. But as more and more letters came to light, Bethge, whom Bonhoeffer had congratulated for his ability to see with discernment, came to recognize this literature as having interest beyond the original circle. So the collection was expanded and the book appeared in 1951. Bethge wrote in a later edition that the passing of a quarter century had left fewer familial reasons to restrict the message to the private zone.

As he made editorial decisions, Bethge also seemed not to be fully confident about the validity of this genre of theological writing, since it was so fragmentary and structurally disjointed. High-level philosophical discourse on one page, he found, would be followed on the next by chatty counsel about Bethge's forthcoming marriage or somber talk about the terror of the bombings of Berlin, some of which rocked the prison the night before Bonhoeffer was writing about it. (Pockmarks left by those bombs are still visible in the walls of Tegel prison.) Credit Bethge: it took profound acts of empathy, imagination, and risk to picture potentially influential, even path-breaking, theology issuing out of such contexts. "Never mind," the emergent reading public in effect kept responding, and, better, "give us more." The episodic and broken genre of the fledgling book seemed to match the moment in the larger culture, where old traditions had been savaged and reasoned discourse often went unheard or was even abandoned. It was time for new starts.

The finished book did not consist only of letters. Being conscientious about following up the Bonhoeffer trail and while serving as a student chaplain after the war, Bethge collected poems and papers. This work also led him to travel to Union Theological Seminary in New York, which Bonhoeffer had attended in 1931 and to which he had returned briefly in 1939.

Bethge followed this trip with pastoral work in the London parish that Bonhoeffer had served early in World War II. Critics agree that Bethge through this career as editor and eventual biographer was faithful to his subject, but that he also possessed the inner resources never to be adulatory or subservient. He did, of course and in the nature of things, subordinate his own writing interests in order to promote and present his late friend's work. Looking ahead: the climactic but far from the final acts in his revised career occurred in 1967 when he published the biography of Bonhoeffer, a book rich in expositions of his work. The career of *Letters and Papers from Prison* alongside that biography reveals how industriously Bethge served the lore and legend of Bonhoeffer as he dug up the best sources for interpreting the vocation of the late theologian.

While Bethge was being conscripted and trained, Bonhoeffer finally had learned of his own forthcoming indictment. The terms of his imprisonment henceforth became more constricted, but he was still free to write some letters to Maria, The letters to and from her were published with her permission after her death, as *Love Letters.*[7]

As the war progressed, the status of Bethge as an exempt pastor was ever harder to sustain, and it took some string-pulling by relatives of Bonhoeffer, notably his brother-in-law, Hans von Dohnanyi, to develop semifictitious make-work posts in the *Abwehr*. This was an ideal place from which to work because in it one could appear to be loyal to Germany while promoting both Christian mission work overtly and, covertly, the religious resistance network of conspirators and potential assassins. If such a task and status seemed to be and was duplicitous, its working out suggests something of how desperate people of conscience were becoming. It was in this range of activities that Bethge could gain the vision and perspective that Bonhoeffer associated with his ability to see with discernment. Had all the contrivances by sponsor von Dohnanyi not been effective, it is likely that Bethge would have been drafted and sent as cannon fodder to the eastern front—and, alongside the personal tragedy that would have involved, we would have no book.

Fostering Meant More Than Editing

One of the last letters from the prisoner was a virtual passing of the literary baton from Bonhoeffer to Bethge, with whom, he had said, he shared strong spiritual affinity. Testimony followed: "Your gift of *seeing* seems to me to be the most important thing yet it is precisely *how* and *what* you see" that represented a "clear, open and yet reverent seeing."[8] One thinks of Goethe's way of speaking about ordinary seeing versus seeing encapsulated in the word *schauen,* which, we might say, meant *really* to see. Bethge used some of that sense of seeing as he read the letters and came to recognize how important it was to give birth to this book of letters and papers.

He provided generous personal clues as to why his interpreting of Bonhoeffer came to be so appropriate. On one occasion he wrote that he was more than a monitor and transmitter of his friend's writings. He said that before the war interrupted their course and disrupted their common work they had had an advantage "when nearly every day for eight years one has experienced each event" with the other. They had "discussed every thought with each other." He concluded: "Then one needs only a second to know how things are for each other, and actually one doesn't even need this second."[9] After peace came and Bethge could return to familiar circles, he took care of the affairs of widows and other family members who survived the four close Bonhoeffer family members after Hitler's executioners killed them.

The contrast between the exciting contents of the letters and these drab temporary housings impresses those who read the letters and contemplate what prison existence must have been like. Some of the notices look routine and banal. They amounted to little more than requests to family and friends for books, pages of which Bonhoeffer literarily consumed. Pages in other books, when returned, were full of faint pencil marks under sequences of letters of the alphabet. When scanned page by page and then connected by decipherers, they turned out to be revealing sentences. Through all the prison writings we learn little of what any Tegel prisoners knew from the outside world about how the German cause was going. The fate of those imprisoned was connected to the progress or lack of progress of the war, now that Hitler was wasting the youth of a nation and seeing the end of his Reich in its conflict with Soviet Russia to the east while acting in denial as Allied forces began to make clinching moves from the west. Instead, in many letters, we do learn something of Bonhoeffer's taste in music, literature, and bird-watching, commented on in passages that reveal how he kept his sanity and, as some letters show, even on many days, his apparent good cheer.

Subsequent Years

Bethge's work on occasion took him to the United States. Eberhard and his wife Renata personally spread word of the letters a few years after they were published and discussed their promise on a new continent, in the Alden-Tuthill Lectures at Chicago Theological Seminary in 1961. There I first met Bethge, and, while John de Gruchy did not attend, it was these lectures that informed and tantalized de Gruchy enough for him to go to Europe to establish contact with Bethge, whose biographer he later became. De Gruchy wrote that in the Chicago lectures Bethge provided the framework for many of the successive interpretations. De Gruchy foresaw developments on the horizon that would wrench the theologian's legacy out of the domain of theologians, pastors, and seminarians and thrust it into a larger public domain. That day was not far off.

I hope a personal intrusion here can be forgiven. It was that hearing and meeting of Bethge that led me to respond when a publisher asked for a collection of essays by a variety of theologians who were taking Bonhoeffer into account. The seven contributors, whose chapters are still on occasion cited, contributed to *The Place of Bonhoeffer*, an edited work that is often pointed to as the first such book-length symposium on Bonhoeffer in America. While I have read *Letters and Papers from Prison* through the years and commented regularly on the author, I did not become a "Bonhoeffer scholar" but remained a historian who enjoyed locating him in the story of modern Christianity.[10]

When *Letters and Papers from Prison* was published and as it attracted interest in selected circles, Bethge found his pastoral vocation enlarged as he became also an untiring editor. Seven years before we met him on his first Chicago visit, a study conference of Finkenwalde alumni dealt with "newness" in theology, thanks to the letters and papers. Conferees subsequently produced five volumes called *Die Mündige Welt* between 1955 and 1963. Some parts of these books were translated and appeared in an English version, *World Come of Age*, published in London in 1967.[11] Experts on the subject formed an International Bonhoeffer Society, which held ten International Bonhoeffer

Congresses, beginning in Kaiserswerth in Germany in 1972 and convening as recently as 2008 in Prague. In its early years, the society and the congress included numbers of people who had known Bonhoeffer from before the war and Bethge from soon after it. Today, two generations later, their interest and energy have not flagged.

Bethge endured in his role, living into his nineties. Through the years he responded to admirers of the letters and of his work, to critics, and to those who, he suggested, misinterpreted the book. As with lives of persons, so with lives of books: friends and foes line up to comment on the legacies, while those at some distance profit from their observations and contentions. Thus, we shall see, as he read some of the more radical essays about his new role, he called some of the responses dangerous. They were so, he thought, because many essayists lost the anchor or pivot that held and directed Bonhoeffer himself. He recognized in many a fundamental misinterpretation of the letters, which, he charged, led readers to think that an optimistic analysis of the contemporary scene was central to Bonhoeffer's thought. No, the pivot of all of Bonhoeffer's liberating analyses was Christology.

Editor and biographer Bethge was foreseeing a fundamental divide among those who dealt with the life of the book. On the one hand were those who saw continuity between the Bonhoeffer they had known before the publication of *Letters and Papers from Prison* and the person who emerged in those letters;

they were now challenged by him, though still in his familiar context. On the other were those who picked up on some late themes in the letters, themes that had been useful in Eastern Europe when Christians were seeking ways to live in a secular, atheist, and anti-church society. They also had counterparts among some radical theologians in the United States and sometimes in what was then called the "Third World."

To understand why Bethge saw the latter trends as dangerous demands an elaboration of themes from the late letters. Their existence poses the question: is *Letters and Papers from Prison* one book or two, written by a Christian scholar who was also of one mind or two? Answers to such questions frame the latter-day stories in the biography of this book.

The Decisive Turns

Readers who never would have bought books of systematic theology, for which there is a small market, may well have merely stumbled upon the book named *Letters and Papers from Prison* or had it recommended to them by a friend. It is likely that if they had opened and begun reading, they would very quickly have been drawn in to the human drama of the early pages. What they could not have anticipated is that after 278 pages in the familiar 1978 edition or 360 pages in the definitive version, which includes letters dated up to April 26, 1944, comes a sequence beginning with a historic comment in a letter to Bethge dated April 30, 1944. After quiet reflections on prison life and business-like notes to his family and friends, Bonhoeffer wrote to tell Bethge what was on his mind and to get theological reactions.

Several years later, when Bethge published the letters, these later statements forced all his readers to reappraise Bonhoeffer. While doing so, many of them embarked with him on spiritual ventures they cannot have anticipated. For them, a new world of interpretation was opening. Some exploited this charter to advance their own viewpoints. Others rejected them as too uncharacteristic of Bonhoeffer and too disturbing to the faithful, while most used them somehow or other to revise their own approaches to faith and culture.

The First Theme of the Book:
Quiet Suffering Revealed

For the most part, distanced as he was from libraries, faculty rooms, colleagues, and conferences, which are the usual stimulants to inquiry and writing, the prisoner was on his own. Only insensitive readers could fail to be moved by the early letters, for they revealed a soul from whom they could learn about captivity and freedom, betrayal and faithfulness, isolation and community. One may have gotten at most a few inklings from them that something portentous was fermenting in the author's mind. Those pages would not have provided the kind of text that would inspire and inform conferences, activist groups, religious vocations, seminary courses, theological and churchly conflict, and shelves full of books that take off from Bonhoeffer or try to bring him down. The pages that follow the letter of April 30, 1944, however, did all of that.

In a sense that fictional reader whom I invented at the beginning of this book, the one who picked up the prison letters volume in a junk box, would have gone home with two books for the price of one. On the pages of these earlier letters readers were drawn in at once to the world I have described. It was a scene of prison halls and cells, of blankets that stank and through which the prisoner feared disease would be spread, of a neighbor in a nearby cell crying the night away, of breakfast in the form of dry bread thrown into the cell, and the absence of any word of greeting by the bread-tosser. They would read on, following reflections on solitary confinement and then limited human contact written by the arrested man. As the letters mentioned, he tried to find balance and focus by establishing disciplines, including doing physical exercises, and finding relief during enjoyment of occasional smuggled gifts. And he prayed.

At times Bonhoeffer had found ways to serve informally as a pastor who counseled other prisoners. As he awaited his own trial, he was occasionally able to learn a bit of what was going on outside, thanks to the efforts of a relatively benign prison commandant, Captain Walter Maetz. Meanwhile, the prisoner ordinarily experienced an unwelcome solitude, but one that allowed for reading and writing.

There were hints of drama. For a while there had been some pointless talk of a daring but hopeless escape plan, as there so often is among the confined. Reports of the death of friends on battlefields kept reaching him. One day he noted a scratch on the wall, an anonymous graffito: "In a hundred years it'll all be over." "It" was over much sooner than that, but, of course, Bonhoeffer could not foresee what was to come. Meanwhile, familiar spiritual disciplines sustained him as he read and memorized scriptures while he wrote of feeling the absence of sacramental life and company. He composed some poems that many cherish today. As he read and reread letters from Maria, he reflected in writing on the subject of earthly desires. Recreationally, at times he could play chess and listen to music.

Little details stand out and inspire in the reader wishes for more. Thus on one occasion Bonhoeffer reported that he heard an anti-Semitic remark, something that cannot have been rare in a German prison or out of it. Bonhoeffer reported that upon hearing it he dropped his contact with the anti-Semitic speaker. Certainly, we would like to have read more. The reader may note that there is little in the book to satisfy the curiosity of those who are eager to hear of the story of Jews in the contexts of what was said or heard in prison. They would find little or nothing in the letters about realities we associate with the Holocaust today. Prisoners could not have been informed about the Jews in any detail. In subsequent decades the public has become rightfully engrossed in stories of the Holocaust. That public also remains in pursuit of the stories of Christian and Jewish relations in Nazi Germany, but there has to be little for them to go on here.

This mention prompts a paragraph whose presence violates the self-imposed rules of the game in which

I am writing the biography of a single book and not a whole life. Outside the figurative borders of these letters and in earlier years, Bonhoeffer had demonstrated concern for Jews, who were to become victims of genocide in the years of *Letters and Papers from Prison*. He had identified with the Confessing Church and, with many of the clergy members, had rejected a despicable Aryan Clause in Nazi-directed church policy. Most Protestant and Catholic clerics were silent when the Nazi leadership imposed its anti-Jewish strictures on churches. Some who admire Bonhoeffer for his courage and witness have wanted him to be declared a Righteous Gentile, a designation awarded individuals who gave their life to identify with or who died for Jews. Others have expressed disappointment, bewilderment, or deeper criticism because he was not cited. One can say that he was "a product of his times," one in which even the better German church leaders did little to understand, support, or identify with Jews. Or one can note, properly, that he also transcended those times more than did most clergy. Whatever one makes of controversies on this front, it has to be said that these letters, which were written under censorship and, if discovered and read, might threaten the lives of people mentioned in them, did not allow Bonhoeffer an occasion to develop thoughts on Christian–Jewish relations.

His reflections on many subjects did, however, grow deeper as the months of confinement passed. An implied message in his letters was counsel to "live each day as if it were your last," a cliché that became vivid as he pondered his circumstances. He had long revealed his reflective side, as he did in the searing autobiographical passage inserted among the papers at the beginning of the book.[1] In it he had asked, "Are we still of any use?" He could not definitively or emphatically answer with a "yes" for his generation, his friends, or himself. His way of life suggested that that question at the heart of a Christmas message given to three friends in 1943 remained a question. We know of this message itself and learn how it survived, because one copy was later found after it had been partly hidden under a roof beam at his parents' home.

Affirmatively, in the letters from prison that followed, the first in the book, there are signs that the old piety lived on. The author almost reflexively lived by the rhythms of the church year and recited classic Lutheran hymns to himself in his cell. His family, his mother especially, needed comfort; "Who would have thought it possible that such a thing could happen to you!" she wrote in agony. "We are trying to come to terms with our old concepts of an arrest being a shameful thing. This only makes life unnecessarily difficult."[2] The letters to this point mingle the humdrum with minor dramatic nuances.

Another Adventure Entirely: The Late Letters

Then comes the letter of April 30, 1944, which jars the attentive reader and opens the door to another life in this book. In it, though anticipated but certainly not developed before, is the question Bonhoeffer pressed on himself and, one presumes, on all aware Christians or anyone who wants to make sense of the believers they know. "What keeps gnawing at me is the question, what is Christianity, or who is Christ actually for us today?" ("*wer Christus heute für uns eigentlich ist.*")[3] This query opened a reflection on what became a famed and controversial definition of what Bonhoeffer called a *world that has come of age*, a culture or civilization that he thought had reached maturity or adulthood. Some read the question and the few sentences that provided a context for it as signaling an epochal turn in the outlook of thoughtful people:

> What might surprise or perhaps even worry you would be my theological thoughts and where they are leading . . . . What keeps gnawing at me is the question, what is Christianity, or who is Christ actually for us today? The age when we could tell people that with words—whether with theological or with pious words—is past, as is the age of inwardness and of conscience, and that means the age of religion altogether. We are approaching a completely religionless age; people as they are now simply cannot be religious anymore. Even those who honestly describe themselves as "religious" aren't really practicing that at all; they presumably mean something quite different by "religious."[4]

The word "us" in the key question sounds limiting. Did it mean German Protestants who would look beyond the war, Western Christians who would look beyond the moment, or the one-third of the human race identified with the name of this Christ? The question needed a context, which Bonhoeffer provided a few lines later:

> But our entire nineteen hundred years of Christian preaching and theology are built on the "religious a priori" in human beings. "Christianity" has always been a form (perhaps the true form) of "religion." Yet if it becomes obvious one day that this "a priori" doesn't exist, that it has been a historically conditioned and transitory form of human expression, then people really will become radically religionless—and I believe that this is already more or less the case (why, for example, doesn't this war provoke a "religious" reaction like all the previous ones?)—what does that then mean for "Christianity"? . . . How can Christ become Lord of the religionless as well? Is there such a thing as a religionless Christian? If religion is only the garb in which Christianity is clothed and this garb has looked very different in different ages—what then is religionless Christianity? . . . The questions to be answered would be: What does a church, a congregation, a sermon, a liturgy, a Christian life, mean in a religionless world? How do we talk about God—without religion,

that is, without the temporally conditioned pre-suppositions of metaphysics, inner life, and so on?[5]

Two months later he added a description of the world around him, or of the emergent world in general: "My starting point was that God is being increasingly pushed out of a world come of age, from the realm of our knowledge and life, and, since Kant, has only occupied the ground beyond the world of experience."[6]

From the time Bonhoeffer's words were published and noticed to the present there have been book-length debates over the meaning of *Mündigkeit*, adulthood, of the world having "come of age." Where did he get his angle of vision, his basis for measurement? He gave scholars who read him some clues. But, on first reading, one asks: could the prisoner have foreseen how many aspects of religion were disappearing from his Western European and North American scene and ethos? Through the years I have been asked by people who knew of my interest in Bonhoeffer and my reporting on religion and secularity: did his tiny prison cell and his confinement keep him from becoming aware of the startling growth of religion, and specifically of Christianity, in the southern world, the less developed world, and selectively elsewhere? Did he overlook the disguises and adaptations, the improvisations and inventions of the concept and phenomenon of "religion," also as a penumbra for Christian faith in the literate and rich post—Christian world?

The returns are not yet in on what such contradictory trends portray. One set of respondents went with Bonhoeffer all the way into that described as a world that has come of age and were glad that they could cite him for making so much of the inevitable secularization they experienced and would advance. Bonhoeffer had much more to say on the subject, but this phrase was enough to raise puzzlement and ire among many Christians, to induce others who had been informed and moved by Bonhoeffer's earlier writings to jump ship, and to encourage some critics of religiosity to explore humanistic approaches to Jesus, or to forget about Jesus and church as did so many contemporaries.

Even more drastic than his musings about a world that has come of age were his pointings to what he and many followers envisioned as "religionless Christianity." He also posed fresh questions about Christ's identity in the new situation, and a couple of times he went even further: Since even *talking* about God had become problematic, Bonhoeffer thought, so had *God*. The prisoner in later letters dealt with that issue in ways that Bethge remembered from his first reading of them as being "explosive." Bonhoeffer dropped more clues as he carried on his questioning. If "metaphysics" and "inwardness" or "the inner life" could no longer produce God as an a priori for faith, he thought that Christian witness itself had to take new directions. Bonhoeffer did not turn atheist or become a simple agnostic. He was too good a theologian to think one could prove the existence *or* the nonexistence of God.

But, he had to ask, could the old God-hypothesis itself work any longer? He offered an upsetting observation that further represented a new chapter in the biography of what became his book:

> As a working hypothesis for morality, politics, and the natural sciences, God has been overcome and done away with, but also as a working hypothesis for philosophy and religion (Feuerbach!). It is a matter of intellectual integrity to drop this working hypothesis, or eliminate it as far as possible. An edifying scientist, physician, and so forth is a hybrid. So where is any room left for God? . . . And we cannot be honest unless we recognize that we have to live in the world—"*etsi deus non daretur.*" [The best contextual translation of the Latin would be "Even if there were no God."][7]

Then, to complicate matters, he added a paragraph that sounds contradictory to what had gone before, but which provided a clue to a charter for fresh theological thinking. Again, we have to live in the world "even if there were no God":

> And this is precisely what we do recognize—before God! God himself compels us to recognize it. Thus our coming of age leads us to a truer recognition of our situation before God. God would have us know that we must live as those who manage their lives without God. The same God who is with us is the God who forsakes us. (Mark 15:34) The same

God who makes us to live in the world without the working hypothesis of God is the God before whom we stand continually. Before God and with God, we live without God. God consents to be pushed out of the world and onto the cross; God is weak and powerless in the world and in precisely this way, and only so, is at our side and helps us. Matt. 8:17 make it quite clear that Christ helps us not by virtue of his omnipotence but rather by virtue of his weakness and suffering! This is the crucial distinction between Christianity and all religions.[8]

At times Bonhoeffer would express his emergent theology through prayers and hymns. Analysis and appreciation of the life of this book are not limited to the work of theologians, historians, philosophers, or literary critics. Students of poetry and singers of songs not only analyze but reprint and sing some of what he wrote. It would carry this biography far afield if I indulged myself and did much with the poetry, so this one sample will have to suffice. It is a poem, "Christians and Pagans," which he sent to Bethge, who included it among the papers. It matches the accent on the weakness and suffering of God, of God in Christ:

People go to God when they're in need,
plead for help, pray for blessing and bread,
for rescue from their sickness, guilt, and death.
So do they all, all of them, Christians and heathens.
People go to God when God's in need,

find God poor, reviled, without shelter or bread,
see God devoured by sin, weakness, and death.
Christians stand by God in God's own pain.

God goes to all people in their need,
fills body and soul with God's own bread,
Goes for Christians and heathens to Calvary's
    death
And forgives them both.[9]

In fairness to Bonhoeffer's poetry, since translations of poetry can be only partly satisfying, here is the
original:

Men gehen zu Gott in ihrer Not,
flehen um Hilfe, bitten um Glück und Brot
um Errettung aus Krankheit, Schuld und Tod.
So tun sie alle, alle, Christen und Heiden.

Menschen gehen zu Gott in Seiner Not,
finden ihn arm, geschmäht, ohne Obdach und
    Brot,
sehn ihn verschlungen von Sünde, Schwachheit
    und Tod.
Christen stehen bei Gott in Seinen Leiden.

Gott geht zu allen Menschen in ihrer Not,
Sättigt den Leib und die Seele mit Seinem Brot,
stirbt für Christen und Heiden den Kreuzestod,
und vergibt ihnen beiden.

Bonhoeffer, though confined and isolated, could
well picture the turmoil that the paradoxes in a poem

like this or the observation from the letter just quoted
could cause if they were circulated among the unpre-
pared. Years later an American pastor who is a leader
in the International Bonhoeffer Congress, John Matthews, quoted four words from this letter and made
of them a book title: "*Anxious souls will ask* what room
there is left for God now . . . ."[10] This was an anxiety
that Bonhoeffer thought had to be met with absolute
honesty. In his mind, living by faith in Jesus without
relying on what was pious, metaphysical, or a prop of
"the inner life" meant that one must reconceive—in
Bonhoeffer's world, on biblical grounds—a different
ascription of Jesus. He chose Jesus as "the man for
others."

"Anxious Souls Will Ask": "Nervousness" along the Trail

That American pastor was right: anxious souls *would*
ask, and *did* ask, about observations and proposals
like all of these, while scholars of religion debated and
still debate the first of the observations, the notice
about "the world that has come of age." Through the
years it often happens that I meet critical admirers of
Bonhoeffer who know that I have done some work on
him. Then I become a sort of "anxious soul" on the
spot as they grill me: if you are a Christian, does that
mean you celebrate the secular world "come of age,"
choose to be religionless, are ready to act and think

also "even if there were no God"? Well, yes, comes out to be my answer, after I have given a long reply full of hedges and qualifications before that answer becomes clear. Philosopher Anthony Flew used the phrase about a certain philosophical proposition, that it "died the death of a thousand qualifications." My questioners might think my affirmation was similarly dying.

And yet . . . and yet. All the while during our conversation such questioners and I are aware, as we look around us, of what appear to exist as *un*anxious souls, or at least souls who are not anxious about these motifs and questions of Bonhoeffer's. They have little at stake in all of this if they are not Christian. But if they are Christian they may relish the Bonhoeffer criticisms of conventional piety and metaphysics and prattle.

Clearly, these various sets of people are reflecting and drawing on biblical, Christian, historical, and theological strands that Bonhoeffer's letters and papers prompt. Was he, with naiveté, exuberance, or superficiality, working his own way out of attachment to Christ, whom he chose to call "the man for others," and then to every form of the church and what gets designated as religion? So powerful have been the discussions of these poles that they have generated a Bonhoeffer industry, which we can only sample as we pursue the life of this book.

For instance, on the decisive concept of "religionless Christianity," one can turn with some confidence to a voice that belonged to a newer generation of Bonhoeffer scholars, Ralf K. Wüstenberg, who used the word "religionless" in the subtitle of his *A Theology of Life*: *Dietrich Bonhoeffer's Religionless Christianity*. He published it in 1998, almost a half century after Bethge's publication of *Letters and Papers from Prison*. Identified on the cover as a vicar of the Lutheran Church in Hessen/Nassau Germany and a research fellow at the University of Heidelberg, Wüstenberg has gone on to a career at the University of Flensburg in Germany. He came with endorsements from leaders of the senior Bonhoeffer scholar generation, notably Clifford J. Green, H. Martin Rumscheidt, and Geffrey B. Kelly among the North Americans. What did this author, who now had the benefit of a longer perspective, think of "the world that has come of age" and "religionless Christianity"?

Wüstenberg found it necessary to write because he looked out on a bewildering landscape strewn with vivid and often contradictory descriptions of the author of the prison letters.[11] I will omit the names of the authors to whom Wüstenberg is referring and simply cite what he put in quotation marks to summarize their views of him. Bonhoeffer was, variously, "atheist," "secularist," "an elemental believer," a "religious naturalist," the "father of the death-of-God theology," a "Gnostic," a "language analyst," a "hermeneutician," a "conservative," or a mere "recipient." To balance all of that, Wüstenberg quoted authors who warned against letting "religionlessness" degenerate into a slogan or allowing it to become a "springboard" upon which virtually any theology might articulate itself. It certainly did serve as such a springboard, and the ambiguities and contradictions among interpreters helped assure a lively biography of a book—of theology, no less!

For the most part, as we already observed, the philosophical references in the book could not have been based on fresh research by a prisoner at Tegel. Those photographs that survive of Bonhoeffer's cell at Tegel depict no shelves or reveal little room for books at all, and the prisoner had no access to a library. He was able to ask for and sometimes did receive a very few cherished books. They are volumes that become important to readers of the prison letters because what Bonhoeffer read during the months when he was formulating "world that has come of age" and "nonreligious interpretations of faith" can help clarify some of the still raw but fresh ideas he was entertaining. Some of these references in particular have helped scholars make their own kind of sense of his apparently paradoxical provocations.

Wüstenberg condensed the thesis of his book in an essay in a collection, *Bonhoeffer for a New Day*,[12] which was made up of papers from a conference at Cape Town in 1996, when he was still at Humboldt University in Berlin. That academy had earlier served as one of the six theological faculties sanctioned by the aggressively atheistic regime of East Germany. From there, as we shall see, Professor Hanfried Müller, with colleagues who were devoted to Marxist interpretations, adapted the meaning of the letters and made them satisfying to those who were sympathetic with or who even represented the regime. Few or no traces of that radical outlook colored what Wüstenberg wrote for the Cape Town conference on Bonhoeffer, a half decade after the fall of the Berlin Wall and also after what we might call the liberation from Marxist ideology at Humboldt University. To the core, his interpretation is Christological—a term that I will define later—and he insisted that Christology came to the fore all the while that the conventionally conceived God was receding.

In introducing his own terms, Wüstenberg insisted, "Bonhoeffer wanted to provide a hermeneutic, whereby Christ would become Lord of the world again."[13] With this instrument, Wüstenberg said, Bonhoeffer could not be seen as an "atheist," "secularist," or "the father of the God-is-dead-theology," as some were to see him, nor, at the other extreme, could he be written up or written off as having a "religious nature," as other camps of critics spoke of him. Such misuse of terms, he contended, tells more about the outlook of those who wrote in this way than about Bonhoeffer himself, who "was in fact, made a participant in the debate about secularism."

Philosophical Texts in the Background

To interpret this interpretation, the essayist retraced Bonhoeffer's writings back to the beginnings of his career, but these texts would not be available to someone like our imagined reader who has only the Tegel writings before him or her. It is within the letters and papers themselves that Bonhoeffer provided a clue to his new thinking. Of course, as a reader of the towering theologian Karl Barth, he was familiar with his elder's paradoxical-sounding concept of *Religion als Unglaube*, "religion as unbelief." He would draw upon and develop that idea in his own critiques in the letters after April 30, 1944.

Now we hear the source question for Wüstenberg, who knew that Bonhoeffer's final probing ideas did not leap out of his brain fully formed: "But what is the origin of Bonhoeffer's thoughts on religionlessness?" The answer for Wüstenberg was this: however these developed in the personal spirituality of this theologian, literarily they grew out of what he convincingly documents as having been prompted by "the philosophy which Bonhoeffer adopted." He singled out two philosophers, one the German Wilhelm Dilthey and the other, Dilthey's student, Spanish thinker José Ortega y Gasset. On the trail of these, we read that on October 4, 1943, Bonhoeffer asked his parents in a letter from Tegel for Ortega's book of essays on "history as a system," and then on January 14, 1944, he wrote them that he was "enjoying Dilthey." On March 2, 1944, he asked for a specific reference, Dilthey's *Weltanschauung und Analyse des Menschen seit Renaissance und Reformation*.[14]

This tracing of the life of a book is demanded because of a shift in genre within it at this point.

We picture the experience of many readers who had been drawn to the letters by stories of their author's death, his testimony against Hitler, and his complex if brief life. Many pastors through the years have told of how the book had been decisive in bringing them to seminary and ministry. At the same time it is also very much a layperson's book, since its theology is dispensed through many short and highly personal bits of correspondence. Bonhoeffer has been the subject of novels, movies, plays, and television programs, which climax in treatments of his last days, most of which we know about mainly through these letters to and from the Tegel prison cell. It may seem distracting to interrupt the flow of them to be drawn to the sometimes arcane and dense writings of a German philosopher of history, as well as those of a Spanish philosopher-journalist-teacher, whose prose style is clear but whose subject matter seems to be a departure from Bonhoeffer's concerns. Yet, the letter-writing theologian *was* a theologian, a very learned and thoughtful one, and to make sense of what he wrote in reflection is best illuminated if we pay attention to what it is on which he reflected. Wüstenberg did just that.

The key word in what he drew from both authors is *historical*, as opposed, for example, to the more familiar word in works of philosophy, *reason*. According to Dilthey's *historicism*, on which Bonhoeffer traded, humans began thinking autonomously from the time of the Renaissance and the Reformation. Since then, Bonhoeffer observed, citing Niccolo Machiavelli, Hugo

Grotius, Galileo Galilei, and others, increasingly they no longer used God as a stop-gap, but began to employ autonomous reason to explain politics, law, and natural sciences. Ernst Feil, another student of Bonhoeffer's writings, noticed that terms the prisoner used to criticize the religious, words such as "inwardness" in theology or "metaphysics" in philosophy, in the present contexts, were derived from Dilthey.[15] In a letter of June 8, 1944, written while we know he was studying Dilthey, Bonhoeffer observed that the early modern thinkers had begun to determine matters without using God as a "working hypothesis," and that "God" was "being pushed more and more out of life, losing more and more ground."[16] Then, instantly, Bonhoeffer added: "The question is: 'Christ and the world that has come of age.'" Along the way he also resurrected and employed the term "religionless," which he had met in Dilthey years before.

In the autumn of 1943 Bonhoeffer had also been reading Ortega, whose thought he found to be dovetailing with Dilthey's as he was formulating his own positions. Both thinkers taught the prisoner that "*history* tells us what humanity is, and from this insight one develops a whole philosophy of life." It was now that Bonhoeffer made another leap as he took off from Dilthey to say "we cannot be honest unless we recognize that we have to live in the world *etsi deus non daretur* [even if there were no God]." Here Wüstenberg almost pounced in his eagerness to bring in Christology: *living* in this world, he writes, for

Bonhoeffer "does not mean 'the shallow and banal this-worldliness of the enlightened, the busy, the comfortable, or the lascivious, but the profound this-worldliness, characterized by discipline and the constant knowledge of death and resurrection.'" Significantly, those last two nouns showed what interpreting life Christologically did to separate Bonhoeffer from his influencers and their mere "philosophy of life." Life thenceforth, notes Wüstenberg, takes on a different meaning; it stops being merely joy and fun. "Life means participation in the sufferings of God in the world. Bonhoeffer reminds us that the Christian shares 'in God's sufferings through' his life."[17]

Many other readers of the decisive pages in *Letters and Papers from Prison* through four decades came to respond more or less the way Wüstenberg did. He took seriously all the book, and he especially traced the philosophical roots of the latter half, which follow seminal letters of April 30 and June 30, 1944. What brought celebrity to the Bonhoeffer book for a time was the set of responses by authors who chose to take literally and with less sense of context than they should have the "explosive" statements that potentially situated Bonhoeffer among the secularist, antireligious, Godless readers who could deal with a humanistic interpretation of Jesus and would appreciate a dismissal of the church.

Bonhoeffer left himself vulnerable to such interpretations, and he just possibly may have begun to clarify his thought in the months before his execution.

Readers may never assuredly and decisively take command of the phrases we are now examining. For beginnings, had Bethge not had to burn some late letters that might have thrown other light on these undeveloped projections, we would know more about how to interpret them. However, Bethge had seen the letters, which were sent to him, and he saw nothing in them that would have left the author simply on the side of the secularizers or that would have resolved all the perplexing issues these surviving letters left. Far from finding the life of this book a premature dead end, however, we discern that the paradoxical themes are what took the book down new paths, which we cannot resist following.

Travels East

The biography of the book *Letters and Papers from Prison*, like most biographies of humans, takes account of its subject's travels. While the book has "gone global," the story of several places where it received controversial responses will provide readers with material on the basis of which they can do their own reckoning. For our purposes, three of these stand out.

First the book traveled east, to the Bonhoeffer homeland, which between 1945 and 1989 became the "East Germany" of the Cold War. The experience there reveals the uses to which themes from the book were put by churches and universities in a Communist-dominated regime and realm. The second destination was the United Kingdom, where liberal or modernist church leaders exploited themes from the book to advance new theologies or strategies for the church. The third stop takes us to the United States, where a small but very visible cast of self-described radicals made what one of them called a "creative misuse" of Bonhoeffer's late letters.

Three expressive figures stand out in these stops along the way, and their stories become virtual case studies. They are Professor Hanfried Müller of Berlin, Bishop John A. T. Robinson of Woolwich, and Professor William Hamilton of Rochester, New York. Müller was the most ideologically consistent Communist commentator. Robinson wrote a small book that made much of the Bonhoeffer letters and gave them unprecedented attention in the English-speaking world. Hamilton was the most articulate spokesperson for a short-lived but much-noticed company of "death-of-God" theologians. It could be said of all three of them and their colleagues what Hamilton once remarked of his circle: "We make a creative misuse of Bonhoeffer!"[1]

These three illuminating examples were regarded as sensational in their time and remain as landmarks in the biography of the book. Focusing on them here might suggest an ambition to create new sensations, but it is too late for that. These authors and the controversies surrounding them have receded too far into the past to startle readers now. I have different motives in choosing them. First, the notoriety they brought did lead publics to hear of a book that might otherwise have escaped notice and, while doing so, also gave cover to quieter but still controversial users of the Bonhoeffer book. Second, the accents of all three cannot be written off as having been beside the point.

They could and did rightfully insist that they were drawing on unfinished and provocative themes in the letters and papers, and while doing so they exposed to view issues with which subsequent if quieter scholarly comment necessarily dealt.

Metaphorically, these authors walked on the sharp arête or the cliff's edge of theological speculation, and the ways in which they kept or lost balance tells something about the nature of the rugged landscape Bonhoeffer's late letters left them, on which figuratively they had to climb. Concentrating on them helps the reader understand why so much controversy is associated with the career of this book. Extreme sports—martial arts, mountain climbing, and the like—are not the whole story of athletics, but they help bring less dramatic sports into view. These three are not the most profound respondents to Bonhoeffer, but we remain in their debt, even while they fall ever further into obscurity.

Creative Misuse of Bonhoeffer in the East

As the producer of *Letters and Papers from Prison,* Eberhard Bethge had to travel to keep up with its life, beginning in the East. For a sample of the first directions it took, scholars compare a book by Hanfried Müller, *Von der Kirche zur Welt,*[2] with another, *The Theology of Dietrich Bonhoeffer,*[3] by American theologian John Godsey. They are seen as the pioneer book-length trackings of the published letters. Godsey offered a comprehensive view of Bonhoeffer's theology, while Müller dealt most dramatically with the concept of "the world that has come of age" and what that phrase meant for interpretation and tactics. The two books came from, reflected, and projected vastly different worlds. They demonstrate how provocative and in many ways contradictory were the turns that early on characterized the life of *Letters and Papers from Prison*.

Let Bethge, who had brought the writings from a narrow Tegel prison cell into book form for the wide world, do his own reporting on these projects. "The first book on Bonhoeffer's theology to appear in German, by Hanfried Müller in 1961, is as brilliant as it is biased." It interprets the period in which it was written, Bethge wrote, "as a dead-end from the confines of which Bonhoeffer was at last liberated in prison." A page later he added, "in 1961 Hanfried Müller asserted Bonhoeffer's leap forward into an entirely new worldliness during his time in prison." Bethge appended a comment that Müller's book was "brilliant" but was mainly concerned with "exploiting Bonhoeffer's ideas in the interest of Marxism."[4]

Much less revealing was the contrasting study by American John Godsey. Bethge deemed it "reliable, but over-cautious."[5] Bethge's own biographer, South African John de Gruchy, also paired the two: "It was Müller's contention that the only interpretation of Bonhoeffer relevant for our time was one that built on his radical prison reflections. Living in what was then

Communist East Germany, it is not surprising that Müller's interpretation was distinctly Marxist and stood in marked contrast to that of the American theologian Godsey."[6]

It sounds trite to resurrect in this case a term from the Cold War, when American zealots would name anyone to the left of Thomas Jefferson an "atheistic Communist." The language of such polemics has tended to cast a blight over the adjective "atheism," which can be used without polemics and with conceptual propriety. The East Germany in which *Letters and Papers from Prison* appeared was officially and efficiently described as "atheistic" by authorities there, and as "communist" everywhere.

Bethge had little sympathy for the ideologically Marxist interpretation of Hanfried Müller, but he did show measured respect for the author and recognized his brilliance. Already in 1954 Bethge had brought together alumni from the Finkenwalde seminary to Bethel in West Germany to discuss concepts in *Letters and Papers from Prison.* Then, a year later, he led another gathering at Weisensee in East Berlin, the center of Müller's East German endeavors. Papers from both inaugurated a series called *Die Mündige Welt* (The World Come of Age), published in 1954 and 1955. The Weisensee volume focused on "The Problem of 'Non-Religious' Interpretation." De Gruchy later commented that these two books "set the boundaries for the debate" at the end of what Bethge called "the first wave of interest in Bonhoeffer."[7]

This matrix for later Bonhoeffer interpretation both coincidentally and fatefully matched the geopolitical scene at midcentury. For almost half a century, from the end of World War II in 1945 until the collapse of the Soviet Communist empire in 1990, Christian theologians shared a vision that neatly divided the world into three: West versus East, or the "Free World" versus the "Communist World," with a Third World made up of uncommitted or exploited nations. Christians in the West who viewed the Communist East as anti-Christian and atheist were grounding their vision in facts. Leadership in the Soviet Union *was* totalitarian, dictatorial, imperial in its grasp, and dedicated to suppressing and even stamping out Christian expressions. Priests and ministers, especially if their churches had connections to the West or if they in any way resisted the reach of persecutors, were carefully watched, their work circumscribed by laws and harassing officials, and, by the many thousand, clergy were exiled, imprisoned, or murdered.

The Orthodox Church, about which Bonhoeffer's letters were silent, also a suffering body of believers, survived in the Soviet Union and in some of its satellites. Sometimes it did so covertly and sometimes by openly playing along with the regime. In the Soviet sphere it was not free to speak critically or prophetically or to be open to theological influence from the West. The relatively few exchanges and interactions across the political and ideological lines of East and West were regarded with suspicion by most Christians and political leaders on all sides during what came to be called, universally, the Cold War. The Vatican attempted to keep some lines of communication open, and the World Council of Churches remained as a bridge or a forum. The council included Orthodox as well as beleaguered Protestant churches in the East Zone of Germany, Czechoslovakia, or elsewhere in Central Europe and the Baltic nations. It had to be a muted voice and often represented what in the eyes of many of its Cold Warrior enemies were suspect sets of institutions.

The early appearance of the sensational Müller book was part of a movement or an emphasis that prompted a stirring chapter in the early life of Bonhoeffer's book. Humboldt University, where Müller and his colleagues worked, was a renamed transformation of Bonhoeffer's own alma mater. After its glory years it had suffered a takeover by the Nazis and then, in 1946, by the Communists. They brought it under the strict ideological control of the Socialistische Einheitspartei Deutschland, which forbade dissent.

The East German authorities came to be as savage in their scrutiny of churches and in the suppression of religious freedom as were Soviet leaders. An eye cast on this Germany after 1945 would have revealed landscapes punctuated by church steeples or cityscapes where once-bombed churches were slowly being rebuilt. A declared "freedom of worship" by the regime meant only that church doors were open for services, but their staffs and members were to have no unsupervised public presence. The dreaded Stasi, the secret police, spied and reported on even the slightest suspicion of dissent by the church. When the Stasi records were gradually opened after the Berlin Wall fell in 1989, it became clear that, just as many priests and pastors had been reported on and pursued, so other clergy, as collaborators, sold out to the Stasi. Before 1989, it is true, some of the churches finally became rallying bases for opposition to the Communist government and its ways, but for the most part the churches were silenced and compliant victims.

On such a scene one would expect little notice of the Bonhoeffer letters and papers because they were written by a critic of the very Nazism that the Soviet Union had fought in cataclysmic battles of World War II. They did, after all, issue from the suspect or rejected Christian church. The letters and papers, written by an expressive theologian, presented ideas that, even though necessarily coded to escape censorship, spoke of freedom. They represented what must have appeared to Eastern European censors to be in the very center of the despised Protestant theological tradition. What chance, one might ask, would a book of such a character have in East Germany and among its neighbors? Where would one even be able to buy it? Who would give publicity to a work that might encourage the Christians who still went to church to single this out as reading matter? The Bonhoeffer book was also not the kind of work that would ordinarily appear on secular university reading lists, especially since its contents did not match the standard curricular slots.

The Uses of Bonhoeffer on the Scene

Against all odds, however, the book did find a hearing, and it attracted a number of champions, particularly among that Humboldt faculty. A group of colleagues there had designed a small institute crafted to propagate theology whose accents would be found compatible with some voiced in the Communist regime. The story of how this came about and how it represented one of the more dramatic stories in the life of this book demands some setting of context. Within a dozen years after Bonhoeffer's book appeared in Munich, in West Germany, Koehler & Amelang in Leipzig, East Germany, published Professor Müller's radical elaboration of its main themes as the last part of *Von der Kirche zur Welt*.

The response was significant at once. The improbable reception and expansion of influence into what should have been resistant settings puzzled and, it must be said, often nettled Eberhard Bethge. Diplomatically friendly though he was to East German ventures, he was also clearly anxious when, looking over his own left shoulder, he saw how the life of the book was progressing in what he called "communist countries antagonistic to the West." Bethge soon learned what many an author and publisher has found: launch a book just as you conceive and give birth to a child, and you cannot control all aspects of its or her destiny. As parent, midwife, or teacher, you can do much to nurture and influence the child and will certainly interpret her ways as she begins to make the first tentative and often confusing steps in the larger world. Still, every parent has to know that accidental and contingent events can disrupt the patterns of nurture and throw the offspring off course or, at least, into a very different and unanticipated career. The child will be subjected to all kinds of influences over which her elders have little control, among them those of friends in adolescence, professors in college, comrades in the military, tempters of some sorts, and ideologues of others.

Bonhoeffer through his career and in the letters gave no hint that he was or would be seen as revolutionary or that he could be coopted and claimed by radicals. The names of the bearded God-killers such as Karl Marx and Charles Darwin received at best only passing mention in the letters. Even the atheist theologian Ludwig Feuerbach and philosopher Friedrich Nietzsche appeared only in allusions, the one in parenthesis and the other in a half-dozen lines which the writer devoted more to the philosopher's aesthetic than to his atheistic writings.

If philosophical radicalism was beyond the range of Bonhoeffer's camp and ken, so was political revolution on or from the left. Since in his lifetime the revolutionary appeals and acts from that flank had become captive of totalitarian threats and influences, Soviet

Russian style, there were no lures for this son of an upper-middle-class and marginally aristocratic family. Some critics who appeared in the later life of this book in fact criticized the author for having been too content with bourgeois existence and all its mixed blessings. Plan a revolution by stocking weaponry and teaching guerrilla tactics and you will not find a Bonhoeffer book in the briefcases of the cadres on the left.

One reasonably surmises that to be acclaimed in a newly repressive Germany, which East Germany was, this time under the Communist Left rather than the Nazi Right, would have had to have been a profound concern for Bonhoeffer, whose vocation and outlook were classically theological to the core. He also knew very much of the fist wielded by repressors of religion and the booted heel of oppressors, having seen and felt them through his final twelve years. After his death, in the midst of the Cold War that was being anticipated during World War II and that took shape right after it, he was in every way that mattered a "man of the West." He was a celebrator of many values associated with that West, among these being a liberty that did not begin to be realized in East Germany until after 1989.

The Ideologues on the Left
Were Not Representative

It would be unfair to many leaders and, no doubt, to thousands of congregants if I were to suggest that all energies of the church went into providing dogmatic support for the Communist regime. Concentrating on figures like Hanfried Müller is necessary in the biography of *Letters and Papers from Prison* because in its extremeness it did much to shape the boundaries among respondents, and it illustrates how the book could and did give rise to disparate approaches to theology, the church, and the world. Many pastors and some bishops found ways to do justice to classic Christian doctrine while adapting to life in an uncongenial state. Bishop Otto Dibelius became the best known of these in ecumenical circles, but the most significant figure in the Bonhoeffer tradition was Albrecht Schoenherr. Were this a biography of the man Bonhoeffer, Schoenherr would receive more attention. Since it is the biography of a book, he plays a lesser role.

When this retired bishop of the Berlin-Brandenburg regional church died in 2009, the last of the personal Bonhoeffer circle was gone. He had been in the preacher's seminar at Finkenwalde and retained a friendship with Bonhoeffer as long as they could be in living contact. He is mentioned ten times in the letters, usually in one-word references when the author had occasion to recall the Finkelwalde seminarians, but is rarely cited as a commentator on the letters. He was asked to comment in 1965 on the fortieth anniversary of his mentor's death, and he did so in an article that was published in the United States in the ecumenical magazine *The Christian Century*.

His character shone through in that confessional article, as when he wrote of 1945 as he was becoming an ex-prisoner of war: "My conscience was not clear. I knew that when God asks me, 'Where is your Jewish, your communist, your Polish, your Soviet, your Dutch brother Abel?' I would have nothing to say." So he agreed with the confession of guilt that leaders in the Evangelical Church in Germany formulated within four months after the end of the European war. "Through us, infinite suffering was brought over many peoples and countries." He added ruefully, "Even today not everyone has accepted this confession of guilt." Then came the tribute: "Without [Bonhoeffer's] influence, I do not know what would have become of me." Now, he added: "I regard it as one of my chief responsibilities to pass on to others what I learned from Dietrich Bonhoeffer. I am convinced that he can still be of help to many." This "many" included Schoenherr's fellow East German church people.

Schoenherr wrote of Bonhoeffer that "when there was genuine need, he never spared himself. He was, for example, one of the very few people who in April 1933, after the first Jewish pogroms, publicly intervened on behalf of Jews." Further, "even in 1941, when the 'final solution' was being implemented, he was able on the strength of his contacts to get Jewish people out of the country." The bishop testified to the single-minded focus of Bonhoeffer: "His concern was for the presence of the crucified, the burden-bearing Christ in and through the church. For if Christ is the person for others, then his people must form the church for others" and "the church with others." He added, "this point is particularly important for us in the German Democratic Republic," as they were learning to be the "'Church for others': that is an open church, and it must remain so despite our continuing minority position. When the center is clear, then the boundaries can be open." Schoenherr drew on Bonhoeffer's letter of February 21, 1944, in which he spoke of the dialectic between "resistance and submission," *Widerstand und Ergebung*, the two words in German which we recall became the title of *Letters and Papers from Prison*. That focus, he insisted, "allows us to understand Bonhoeffer's almost frightening calmness in prison."[8]

In 1969 in church struggles over ties to West German churches, Schoenherr drew on such resources, and he continued to do so through 1989 when the Berlin Wall fell. At decisive moments he had been dismissed by Müller and other "progressives" who initiated letter-writing campaigns against those like Schoenherr whom they considered to be moderates. A history such as Robert F. Goeckel's on *The Lutheran Church and the East German State*[9] has to and did show Schoenherr to be a central figure while the "progressives," who drew international attention, tended to be marginalized in the actual life of churches. Still, Müller has to be reckoned with for the way he picked up on the late letters of Bonhoeffer to formulate a strategy not merely for accommodation but for providing Christian ideological defense of the regime. He picked up on Bonhoeffer's reference in one letter to the way Catholic and Protestant historians had come to agree on "the great defection from God" in Europe. This was not something that troubled theologian Müller, who was at home with a regime that encouraged defection. He could write enthusiastically that in the letters we find a "wholly new, secular understanding of history," filled with a "secular and optimistic 'Yes' to human development."[10]

By the time the letters were published the Cold War was intense, and Christians on both sides of the Iron Curtain and the Berlin Wall played high-stakes ideological games at a time when nuclear war threatened. In this close-up scene, some found reason to invoke and to go about variously interpreting this little set of prison letters. The writings had nothing to say about the Soviet Union and Communism itself. Names like that of Lenin do not appear in the letters. Yet in this generation after the war the forces on the left served as "the Other" over against which Western nations and the Christians within them framed their struggles. Conversely, in the German Democratic Republic (GDR) there were good reasons for theologians and politicians to invoke their favorite son Bonhoeffer on their side as much as possible. They did this even as they remained embarrassed by or opposed to his residual Western bourgeois interests and outlook.

This postwar East German state was distinctive since it was the front line where a corner of the earliest and, by 1945, the second-largest Protestant communion in the world, the Lutheran, was thrust into the Communist orbit. Protestants as minorities were present in many subjugated nations, but only in the GDR were the culture and the majority of the population Protestant. Historians see a special poignancy in the fact that these were the regions of Germany where Protestant reformer Martin Luther, who was the focal theologian in Bonhoeffer's heritage and writing, had spent his life and had left profound influences on the political, social, and, of course, religious culture. Here, the Communist regime and the Protestant churches were forced to deal with each other, and they foresaw doing so for a long time to come. Few East Germans, and certainly no theologians like Müller, in 1961 foresaw the fall of the Wall and of German Communism in 1989. They were busy finding ways for Christians to think and live with Communism, and some were drawing on rare figures like Bonhoeffer to attempt this.

The Church Scene in the East

The first four years after the war came to be known in East Germany as "the Antifascist-Democratic Period." For all the compromises made in the years of the Reich, the churches included representatives of the tradition of opposition to Hitler. The new GDR rulers found a need to work with them and even grudgingly granted what historians have united in calling a brief "honeymoon period." Then came the "transformation" on Stalinist lines, 1949–1953, with its evidences of belligerent atheism and greatly increased repression. Yet even then, theological faculties survived in universities such as the Humboldt. However, after 1953 and until 1989 relations between church and Communist regime were more than strained. It is not possible or necessary here to follow all the turns of the screws and twists of the arms among state and church leaders, but for the parts they play in the biography of this book it is to the point to provide an immediate context for understanding Hanfried Müller and his circle.

He and fellow scholars, along with his wife Rosemarie Müller-Streisandt, formed a center of what John A. Moses calls a "Bonhoeffer industry." They began to make the boldest attempts of the day to square some form of Christian witness and service with the practice and many aspects of the ideology of the Communist regime. The members of this circle were not only interested in the survival of theological faculties in the face of an inhibiting regime. They were positively committed to the humanistic side of Marxist and Socialist philosophies. As they became vocal, much of the leadership of West German churches looked on in befuddlement and anger because they opposed such ideologies and were trying to uphold bonds and strands of faith communities across the national boundaries. Their East German critics discerned or alleged that some of these "traditionalists" were trying to restore something of the old privileges for the church from the pre-Nazi past. In their eyes it looked

CHAPTER 4

as if church leaders were contending for what looked like the bourgeois, passive, and submissive church habits that Bonhoeffer had also criticized in exploratory ways in his letters.

Respected bishop Otto Dibelius, a major church leader who was perceived as diplomatic or sometimes in a way complicit, depending on the viewpoint of the observer, did what he could immediately after the war to form bridges among the leaders of the regime and the churches. As the harder line developed in East Germany, he came to be seen by the newer theologians of the East as old-fashioned and bourgeois, as if he were unaware that, as they proclaimed, the world had "come of age" and the old-style church was irrelevant. Others tried bridging experiments. Swiss theologian Karl Barth teamed with a chaplain to students, Johannes Hamel, and with him wrote *How to Serve God in a Marxist Land.*[11] While Barth understandably resented some things Bonhoeffer had said critically about him in the letters, on other topics he still respected the younger man, and his book with Hamel resonated with some Bonhoeffer themes and approaches.

From the Church to the World

Focusing on Müller's book, *Von der Kirche zur Welt*, "from the church to the world," demands more context in this situation of East Germany during the Cold War, which had begun to be intense at the very time

Letters and Papers from Prison was first published. John A. Moses, an Australian scholar who evidenced familiarity with and intellectual understanding of East Germany under Communism, provided a survey that warrants a hearing. In his telling, when Communists claimed the eastern part of Germany in the moments after World War II, they had to determine what to do about religion. All the governmental leaders were and had to be atheists. They were not of the sort that could be described as merely secular or "maturely" postreligious in the styles Bonhoeffer envisioned in his letters. Not casual atheists, they were true believers of a most militant Leninist sort who could not tolerate any God but the god of their philosophy and regime as these made their total claim on people. Yet despite their efforts, through it all the majority of East Germans remained at least nominally Christian, most of them remaining in but seldom attending the state-supported churches that had outlasted the years of the Nazi terror. The Communist leaders had to find some minimal ways to accommodate church members while harassing and inconveniencing them.

The new situation, called "Real Existing Socialism" (RES), worked through a Socialist Unity Party (SED). Seeing Bonhoeffer as a hero for having been in the resistance to Hitler, the SED found him posthumously useful. With the church serving as the only major agency not under direct and total Communist control, the SED formed a Task Force for Church Questions to enforce "total truth" as the Communists saw

it. Bishop Dibelius could see that this regime represented an oppressive threat to the churches, but as a
Lutheran dealing with Lutherans, he also knew how
deep was the commitment of many pastors and laity
to the apostle Paul's writing in Romans 13, that "the
powers that be are ordained of God," and that those
who resist them will receive judgment.

Moses introduced to his readers the regime-friendly
writer Gerhard Winter, who could serve to illustrate
this. On Bonhoeffer's seventy-fifth birthday anniversary, Winter argued that a bourgeois Christian of the
sort Bonhoeffer had been could still be of some use in
an atheistic regime. Communists could not but honor
and be bound to Bonhoeffer, he argued, but he and
his colleagues must move the case along further. Thus,
he wrote: "However, in contrast to Bonhoeffer, *we*
identify the spiritual/intellectual means for the establishment of a society commensurate with human dig-
nity in Marxism-Leninism, the scientific *Weltanschauung* of the working class. So, while we do not ignore
this contrast [with bourgeois Christian thought] we
remain aware of that which binds us."[12]

While Winter advertised Bonhoeffer to Christian
laypeople, theologian Müller worked to help the pastors and other leaders square their acceptance of RES
rule with their preaching of the Christian gospel—
now radically revised though it be. Moses, who has
studied the evidence, believes that few pastors were
deceived by this ploy but recognized how Winter and
Müller had misrepresented and coopted the author of

Letters and Papers from Prison.[13] Because of this use, it would be harder for antiregime people, forces, or movements to make their own hero out of him.

Müller had no qualms about doing so. Taking off from Bonhoeffer's "world that has come of age" theme, he condensed his argument in a chapter for *Die Mündige Welt*, which was soon translated. Thus he made such thought available in the English-speaking West in Cold War times. Scholars point out that he did much of his work before the full text of *Letters and Papers from Prison*, as later generations know it, was available, and the spectrum of critical analysis had not yet offered much perspective. Still, it is worth listening to him for what he embodied. He had first presented his argument as early as November 1956 at a theological faculties seminar in Leipzig. In it he introduced a particular "we" into the Bonhoeffer discourse. "We" are "those . . . who see the necessity of thinking in the light of the revolutionary upheaval of our time, during the course of which central Europe has seen the socialization of society." Müller was brusque about those who had not faced the challenge of change. He posed a new "they" against his "we": "A Protestant church which still bases its thinking on a Christendom which it regards as the definitive ideology for the Western world simply does not know what it is doing. In the midst of these uncertainties, one discovers Dietrich Bonhoeffer."[14]

Because of the climate change that came later with the end of the Cold War in the 1990s and the decline of revolutionary movements in the West, the Müller book holds appeal mainly to historians, not as a manual for change now. Two and more decades after the rending of the Iron Curtain and the toppling of the Berlin Wall it is difficult to convey to newer generations a sense of the climate of the first two decades after Bonhoeffer's book appeared. However, in the decade after the book by Müller was first published, it received notice and evoked East German responses of the sort Bethge was observing—and fearing.

To understand the story of Müller, the mind's eye is put to work recalling scenes from the darkest days. In my case, visits to sites associated with reformer Martin Luther in 1983, his five-hundredth birthday, remain vivid. Only six years later a "silent revolution" was to occur, when worshipers marched from Leipzig churches where Johann Sebastian Bach and other giants had once played organ, so the light of the candles they carried were both a witness to the durability of faith and signs of criticism and subversion. Pastors meanwhile had to be cautious when they spoke. My conversation with one leading pastor had to occur in the town square, far—at least so we presumed—from listening and recording devices. He had to be careful, since staff members of churches, organists, and other pastors might be spying and eavesdropping for the Stasi on a conversation with this or any other American visitor. Consequences for him could be at best inconveniencing and at worst dire.

While church attendance has lapsed through the east of Germany today and in many places one finds nearly empty sanctuaries, quite a few believing citizens worshiped in the 1980s, some, perhaps, not only to praise God but also to defy the regime. In some of the town squares where there were Luther celebration banners, one would sometimes also see a statue of Lenin. One noon, while my company was eating lunch in a Bierstube, being served by spy-shy waiters who could not even risk joshing with guests, I chose to sit in that square and observe the citizenry. Not seldom did I see people of all ages cross a street to avoid walking near the statue of Lenin.

It was in a mix of the sort that I have just described that the churches had to operate, not only in East Germany. Regimes were oppressive in Hungary, Czechoslovakia, Poland, and elsewhere where the teachings of Bonhoeffer, culled and commented upon, were being read. Just as there had been "Confessing" dissenters among church leaders against Nazism, Fascism, and other totalitarian regimes, so now in the East there were a few open dissenters who were often silenced, or quiet dissenters who kept attending to some ministries and witnesses. And then there were the devotees of Communism or, as more of them put it, Socialism.

The pages in my copy of Hanfried Müller's *Von der Kirche zur Welt* are now yellowed and brittle, since the paper stock available in Leipzig in those years was substandard and linenless. Still, appearances deceive: for all its archaic look, it was designed to envision a triumphant future, to project revolutionary ideas, and to help situate them in the social order of a new Communist society. In most of the West the Müller volume should well have been labeled "Handle with Care!" not because of the crisp condition of the paper but for its argument. Still, among those seeking sensation, for whom responsible works like those of Albrecht Schoenherr were overlooked, Müller stood out. In this pattern, American theologian William Hamilton, self-described and often dubbed a "death of God" theologian in 1967, called Müller's the best book yet on Bonhoeffer. Years later, however, it came to be viewed as an antique representing a merely tendentious reading. We can observe this East German appearance as a milestone—though some would say a roadblock—in the course of its life.

In Müller's view, Bonhoeffer by 1944, as revealed in his letters, was free of religious concerns and thus could provide an outlook for the Marxist vision and practice. Ironically, as Müller promoted the ideology, he found himself progressively shunned and even repudiated by those who had known Bonhoeffer's work from before his imprisonment and related that to the writing in the letters.

Bonhoeffer Wrenched from His Past

In the 1960s, a decade of turmoil in the West, Müller was picked up on and in part translated into English for British and American readerships, thanks to a chapter included in an anthology edited by Ronald Gregor Smith. Müller's contribution to Smith's book was "Concerning the Reception and Interpretation of Dietrich Bonhoeffer." Editor Smith defined Müller as neutrally as possible, as someone who saw "the outcome of Bonhoeffer's thought in 'a rational and optimistic atheism which is founded on the freedom of faith' in 'a new picture of history.'" He continued in this stream by saying that Müller located this new picture "quite undialectically in the socialist society, which for him is adumbrated in the East German state" where he was living and teaching.[15]

Müller "undialectically" dismissed the calm and neutralizing interpretations of others which in effect would have shelved the book as in a museum case. No, argued Müller, it is possible to interpret Bonhoeffer "only if we use his heritage as a *living* heritage, and that means only if we continue to suffer, struggle and hope where he has suffered, struggled and hoped." It is likely that many in the West, with their own interpretations, thought they were doing so, but Müller announced that he wanted to lead the reader through the labyrinth of ideology to achieve "the socialization of society."[16] He was sure that it would distort Bonhoeffer, he said, "were we to try to preserve [his heritage] in some neutral, indifferent and apparently objective manner, detached from all controversy without and within the church and the world." He saw a danger, he wrote, that "we" would "slide into a Bonhoeffer orthodoxy." Instead, he wanted readers to take up

Müller's position and deal with the *whole* Bonhoeffer, by concentrating on the *movement* of his thought. There was no question in his mind as to where that development would lead.

There had been few plausible prompts for all such talk in the books Bonhoeffer authored *before* his imprisonment. Müller relied instead on those late and unfinalized *Letters and Papers from Prison.* The question he kept posing was not where Bonhoeffer would have led others had he lived to see the liberation in 1945. It was better, argued Müller, to ask "where would Bonhoeffer stand today?" He recognized in each typical non-Marxist interpreter the temptation at this point to use the theologian's heritage "to further one's own ends, to claim and exploit it for one's own purposes"—precisely what people in the West accused Müller of doing.[17]

If it was difficult to say where Bonhoeffer would stand in a new day, Müller would shift the question to a more congenial place and ask, "Who may legitimately take up Bonhoeffer?" It was all right to talk this way, the East German contended, because Bonhoeffer himself had such a strong interest in the future, the time that was now, the present. Müller celebrated the "fragments, sketches, notes and letters, . . . as evidence of his development" that was going on at the time of Bonhoeffer's death. Müller was not ignorant or deluded; he was instead a scholar in service of an ideology, not so much guileful as driven, sure of his knowledge of where history was going. And even his most severe critics did admit that he was not making up his interpretation out of whole cloth. Bonhoeffer left many loose strands that thinkers in East Germany could pick up. There were several choices available as alternatives to the reading by Müller. All of them had something to say to East Germany and Soviet satellites. For instance, interpreters could agree with Karl Barth, who found the pages of the letters full of "enigmatic utterances." They could follow another major contemporary, Jürgen Moltmann, who looked back and interpreted the new statements in the letter on the basis of earlier syntheses. A third choice was to go along with Oskar Hammelsbeck and others and speak of Bonhoeffer's envisioning of religionless Christianity as "an *ersatz* religion, or of a religion as *ersatz*." One more choice was to "relativize the problem of the letters as 'open questions,' or subjectivize and individualize them by pointing to the frontier situation in which they arose."[18] In the course of the life of the book, all these and other interpretations found supporters and proponents, and we will visit some of them. Müller liked it that in the letters, Bonhoeffer's "world that has come of age" formed "the center of an optimistic way of thinking." Viewing the letters this way prompted Müller to launch another polemic against the bourgeois West:

> The original goal of Bonhoeffer, as with the political powers with which he identified himself [until the time of the prison letters] at this time, was the

rescue of the grand heritage of the Christian West in the face of Nazism. *Here one overlooks, as Bonhoeffer did at the beginning, the fact that Fascism is itself the last stage of decay, the putrefaction of the superannuated bourgeois society in Germany, and cannot be countered by a restoration of this society— for this would be at the same time the restoration of the source of Fascism.*[19]

It was with these interests in mind that, as Müller saw it, Bonhoeffer had joined the movement to kill Hitler and bring Nazism down, but this goal had had to fail. As the new Bonhoeffer was seen to be emerging in the late letters, Müller claimed to discern that he resisted the temptation to be "one of those nihilistic anarchists who thoughtlessly cut themselves off from any continuity with the heritage of history." He was deemed to be, blessedly, "never a counter-revolutionary."[20]

Interpreters agree that the views in the letters were indeed undeveloped, provocative, and in need of later and fuller elaboration. So Müller also did see Bonhoeffer as still a captive of his "stratified" society and observed that even his opposition to Nazism was determined by his heritage—which, Müller had to admit, had been "aristocratic, capitalist, bourgeois, and full of contradictions." Still, at this time, Bonhoeffer seemed to him to be "the last honest Christian Westerner," a half-compliment if we ever read one.[21]

With the Berlin Wall dismantled, the German Democratic Republic an increasingly distant memory, and Müller's thesis, thought provoking as it was, now no longer a central choice for anyone who wants to understand the "world that has come of age" or "religionless Christianity," it may seem a disproportionate use of pages to have spent so many paragraphs on a book that leads to a virtual dead end at a torn-down Berlin Wall. However, with the life of a book as with the life of a person, others can learn as much from what some have called "creative misuse" as one might from staid and unimaginative expressions. The Bonhoeffer revealed in the letters surely understood this, as he took chances and made himself and his book vulnerable to an amazing range of critics. And there were other creative but understandable misrepresentations that helped form other chapters of this biography of a book, following its travels this side of Berlin Walls, Iron Curtains, and humanistic utopias, based on the travels of *Letters and Papers from Prison.*

Travels West

Biographies, life stories of humans, regularly deal with adolescence as a time of restlessness, rebellion, and the search for an identity. Biographies of books like Bonhoeffer's *Letter and Papers from Prison* may by analogy follow similar trajectories and can represent parallel experiences in the same stage. The book enjoyed something like a time of innocence in which seminarians, seekers, and devotionalists, often in isolation from each other, mined it quite simply and perhaps somewhat naively for inspiration and spiritual sustenance. That period was brief. Only four years after its publication, readers who found each other gathered at Bethel in West Germany and a year later in Berlin in East Germany to charter conferences and study groups. They provided leadership in what some called "the Bonhoeffer decade." Out of such beginnings came the burst of activity that brought the book sudden and rare interest, if not notoriety. The parallel goes only so far: a book, of course, cannot be restless or rebellious in search of an identity. It is the readers who have to be thus, as they both take character from and give character to the book.

Early respondents to the controversial letters in the book, as we saw, seized on Bonhoeffer's description of "the world that has come of age." He envisioned the time when the world, which has to mean immediately the world of the West, would attain *Mündigkeit*, adulthood, the coming of age. Many scholars and activists for a time adopted that description of the emergent culture and applied it to cherished causes and ventures. They saw themselves as being on the threshold of such worldly adulthood. Newer generations seem faintly embarrassed to be reminded of that period, which ended in the early 1970s, and turn to other mentors to point the way to more indeterminate futures than the one their academic ancestors foresaw a half century ago.

Retracing steps to that period is necessary for those who want to understand an optimistic dimension of Bonhoeffer's work and to reassess visions of the future. The first step, in an era of globalism, demands cutting down to size the world, as in the "world that has come of age." In the East, the fall of the Berlin Wall and the tearing of the Iron Curtain shattered the dreams of committed ideologues who used some pages in *Letters and Papers* as a charter for a secular society. Their successors in old East Germany might still read Bonhoeffer, but few would look to it to help them plan for any Utopian "world that has come of age" that might still be on the drawing board.

Anglo-America

That leaves "the West," beginning in West Germany and Western Europe, and then moving on to the British Isles and North America, plus many places where their influence is felt, such as South Africa. Thinkers in such locales, addressing many common problems and issues, found and find resource in *Letters and Papers from Prison*. During "the Bonhoeffer decade" it provided agendas, experiment, and even a sense of adventure.

If attention to the book as interpreted by the Marxists was predictable, the dramatic versions of reception, especially in the Anglo-American worlds, were surprising. In the jurisdictions where theologians and other scholars worked, there was little formal governmental pressure to conform to an ideology. True, the ironist might say that such theologians, whom Müller and his colleagues would have called bourgeois, *were* in fact also in service of ideologies. But there was just enough restlessness, rebellion, and search for identity, especially among the newer generations, to lead them to find anything but incentives to complacency in *Letters and Papers from Prison*. In their company was a very diverse groups of people, including emerging cohorts of pacifists, civil rights workers, experimenters with jarring lifestyles in the emerging Age of Aquarius and Jesus People movements, workers against apartheid, and anticolonialists, to be seen as innovators and shakers of temple foundations.

The worlds stereotyped here as East and West were not wholly out of contact and intellectual commerce with each other. The World Council of Churches, the shorter-lived Student Christian Movement, and academic exchange or relief programs assured some mutual influences across Cold War boundaries. After World War II it was still fashionable for advanced members of the theological professoriate and doctoral students in the United States to go to Europe, especially Germany, for research and writing. Names like that of Friedrich Schleiermacher from the nineteenth century and of Karl Barth in the twentieth could be dropped and cited as influences by those in the know. In the years when *Letters and Papers from Prison* undertook its travels around the globe, seminarians in the United States in particular wrestled with what was then called "neo-orthodoxy." This emphasis, accent, or movement colored preaching and teaching, but scholars who study that era find that it did not become a theology that attracted or shaped the thinking and acting of most laypeople. In the eyes of critical academic theologians, church people in the West were less likely to be rebuilding ruined cities, as people in the East of Europe had to do, than fashioning lives that Müller and his colleagues called bourgeois, in newly built suburbs. Preachers of popular gospels of wealth and positive thinking dismissed neo-orthodoxy and German theology in general as "existentialist," gloomy, and out of step. Bonhoeffer, one would have thought, could not have exerted major influence in much of this West.

Despite the odds against any adoption there of Bonhoeffer and his *Letters and Papers from Prison*, his became a familiar name on lay reading lists, and the book served as an inspiration and a manual or charter for planners, dreamers, and activists. Christians were looking for heroes and heroines in an era when new social programs in Britain and the civil rights and antiwar movements in the United States provided a gallery of such figures: Dorothy Day, Martin Luther King, Jr., Mother Teresa, Thomas Merton, and Desmond Tutu were celebrated. In such a climate, Dietrich Bonhoeffer came to be the subject of conferences, his writings provided resources for retreats, and his story came to be told as exemplary.

In the midst of this climate, a moment that was unsettling to many appeared when, especially in England and North America, a group of radical theologians used Bonhoeffer to advance their thinking and their causes. Numbers of them picked up some themes in the later pages of the book of prison letters. They found inspiration for proposals that, they claimed, would turn Western religious thought and particularly what was left of Christianity in new directions. These movements of what were called "radical theology," "death of

God" theology," and some forms of "liberation" theology that drew on Bonhoeffer came and went within less than a decade. However, the story of the attention these drew after they "came" tells much about a questioning church and an unstable academy within a destabilized cultural milieu. This chapter in the life of the book visits this experience and the role of the book for what they tell about Bonhoeffer, his interpreters, his readership, and the rapidly changing cultures where the book was and is being read.

Great Britain

If it was hard to reconceive the climate of the Cold War and of Christian witness under Communism after a wall fell and a curtain tore, it may be just as difficult to recall to new generations the background for the eager reception of *Letters and Papers from Prison* among novelty-seeking radicals. In the British Isles, decline in church participation was increasing after the Second World War to the point that secular motives that could be associated with Bonhoeffer's "world that has come of age" were partly plausible. Conversely, in America, despite the secular ethos surrounding them in the academy, politics, the market, and popular culture, believing citizens were seeing increasing church participation and cooperating in activities that were part of a revival of interest in religion and the promise of more enthusiasm to come. What did Bonhoeffer have to say in these situations?

That readers in England could be shocked, even outraged, over anything a bishop in the Church of England might say seemed strange in a time of growing religious indifference. Yet almost all Bonhoeffer scholars and religious historians agree that when a little book by Bishop John A. T. Robinson, *Honest to God*, appeared in 1963, it was members of the general public, symbolized by the figures who inhabited "cloth-cap England," who were most upset. Why, it was asked, did they care so much about the being and doings of God when most of them rarely dealt manifestly with the things of God? Philosopher Alasdair MacIntyre, viewing the scene, summarized: "The creed of the English is that there is no God and that it is wise to pray to him from time to time."[1]

In this time of indifference and indeterminacy, *Letters and Papers from Prison* suggested to readers that a variety of new cultural options were available. In the decade when fear of extinction by nuclear war was widespread and palpable, it spoke to those who wanted to breathe a spirit of resistance and hope. If reading about how someone like Bonhoeffer in his spirit-killing confinement at Tegel could look beyond the gray clouds visible outside his cell windows and still be seen as an optimist of sorts, they could find examples of the heroic human spirit that could inspire others. Then in the late letters came speculations that provoked thoughts that were seized, exploited, and rendered normative by the small band of innovating theologians who attracted large amounts of space in the secular and religious press alike.

Among and briefly most prominent of them was Bishop Robinson, who in 1963 brought most celebrity to the situation with his cleverly titled book *Honest to God*. In it he implied that the church as known in his time as well as contemporary Christian perceptions fused with piety were dishonest, or at least inauthentic and obsolete. He assumed that younger people brought up on a Christian message and in a churchly community that had struck them as confining at best and restrictive at worst now were looking for a message that held the promise of freedom and authenticity. The letters of Bonhoeffer did this for him.

In its second decade of its public life, *Letters and Papers from Prison* had found its way to the desk of the good bishop, who made headlines with it. The landing of the book in his study inspires notice of the contrasts among receptions for this traveling volume. If in Eastern Europe it would have been difficult to hold high office without professing atheism, in the United States it would have been virtually impossible for anyone to be elected to high or low office while being publicly atheistic. Yet both a bishop in the Church of England and tenured religious studies professors in the United States, some of them card-carrying heirs of church traditions and members of theological faculties, used prompts from Bonhoeffer to expound what critics of the former dismissed as atheism and some advocates of the latter proudly announced as "Christian atheism."

Robinson, the bishop of Woolwich, a biblical scholar of considerable repute and a theologian of somewhat less, confessed that he wrote the book that drew him beyond his specialty while he was dealing with a troubling back, which had brought on a health crisis. He spent many of his 140 pages drawing on theologians Paul Tillich and Rudolf Bultmann, the choices of most liberals for favorite-theologian status in the 1960s. It was the convalescent's briefer takeoff from the then still less well-known Bonhoeffer that came to be regarded as dynamite. In fact, the British translator of Bonhoeffer, Reginald Fuller, called it just that. Himself an important biblical scholar, Fuller conscientiously reported on his thoughts as he was translating the later letters in the summer of 1952. "I remember saying to myself again and again: 'This stuff is dynamite.' I hardly dared read it myself, let alone help to launch it on the English-speaking world." Fuller asked himself, as Robinson did and many readers would, about what to do with key Bonhoeffer explorations, whose content readers can learn from Fuller's context. Among them were: "How can Christ become the Lord, even of those with no religion? ... What is religionless Christianity? ... What is the significance of a Church (church, parish, preaching, Christian life) in a religionless world?" What, the translator and editor went on to ask, should he make of sentences such as "The 'beyond' of God is not that which is beyond our perceptive faculties.... God is the 'beyond' in the midst of life"?[2]

Fuller accurately reported that when the Bonhoeffer book appeared, it was seen first as "an interesting piece of spiritual biography," since people by the time this translation was appearing knew of Bonhoeffer's fate: "Here was the last will and testament of a twentieth-century martyr." Already by then, however, Fuller added, the book was taking on a new life, no longer to be regarded as a simple diary of a martyr, in letter form. He pointed to perceptive Princeton professor Charles C. West, who had written in *Theology Today* already in January 1954 that Bonhoeffer had "left to posterity a prospectus and a sense of direction which may well lead us beyond the conflicts of Barthian and liberal theology, and beyond the estrangement of Church and world." Still, referring to two surviving movements, Fuller noted that, remarkably, "the theological world, however, for the time being continued on its own sweet way, still dominated by neo-orthodox and 'revelational positivism.'" The latter was a confusing term Bonhoeffer used on an occasion when he criticized Karl Barth. It took ten years for the dynamite of which Fuller spoke to explode in Britain and America, and when the explosion came, he wrote, "it was far more devastating than I had anticipated in the Alps in 1952"—where he had been doing the translating.[3]

Bishop Robinson's Provocative Reading

By the time Robinson took Bonhoeffer's themes and ran with them, many in Britain had been reading the book and taking the provocative passages in stride, reading and interpreting them in their original context. Here and there in journals from the period one reads critical comments in book reviews or articles that noticed, or were mildly puzzled by, concepts such as "the world that has come of age" or "religionless Christianity." The situation changed with that dynamite charge of Robinson's short book. We can get another perspective on this from a report in the autobiography of John de Gruchy, an authority on the subject. He was to put Bonhoeffer's writings to work in the South African struggle against apartheid, and he became a leader in Bonhoeffer congresses and book publishing. Professor de Gruchy tells of how the shock of the book and the controversy hit him.[4]

I can key into his recall because I shared an experience with him and a roomful of others. In a chapter on "Being Secular," he tells how in 1963 he was crowded with other graduate students in the Commons Room at the Divinity School of the University of Chicago. There we heard Robinson expound his *Honest to God*. That little book at the moment spoke to de Gruchy, he confessed, and to other young pastors who were "disenchanted with a Christianity that seemed out of touch." Those were upsetting and creative times, de Gruchy remembered, since the civil rights movement in the United States, the struggle against apartheid in South Africa, and Liberation Theology in Latin America were leading him and others to explore what "being secular" might mean for Christians. His own evangelical faith, de Gruchy confessed, made transition difficult.

In 2006 he took a long look back to "those heady times and discussions," admitting later that much of the talk of those years had been voguish, and noting that by the time he wrote, support for Robinson's book was seen to have been part of one passing fad. Like many another fair-minded observer, de Gruchy did not put all the blame for confusion confounded on those who ran with Bonhoeffer's vision. He wrote an at least implied criticism of Bonhoeffer's vision of "the world that has come of age" as the imprisoned letter-writer had projected it into a broadly secular epoch. Instead of the postreligious adulthood envisioned in the letters, things turned out, as de Gruchy saw it, that intense or ecstatic movements like Fundamentalism and Pentecostalism or the liturgies of Eastern Orthodoxy and Roman Catholicism held lures for more people than one's "being secular" as a Christian ever could have for others.

After presenting an informed reflection on the way "the secular" and "the religious" interacted in the near half-century after Robinson spoke, de Gruchy came back to provide his own answer to a question he had posed in the Bonhoeffer tradition. The imprisoned letter-writer, he reflected, had been rejecting "not the spirituality of genuine faith and prayer, but the kind of religion that is individualistic, ego-centric and inward looking, based on a metaphysical view of the world largely discredited by science." While de Gruchy did not try to address all the issues Bonhoeffer raised, he came to the point on one of them. Bonhoeffer wanted to start, he wrote, "from the premise that God shouldn't be smuggled into some last secret place, but that we should frankly recognize that the world, and people, have come of age, that we shouldn't run man down in his worldliness, but confront him with God at his strongest point."

De Gruchy was not at all a slave of devotion to Robinson or Bonhoeffer. In fact, for all that the German theologian had influenced him, the South African was convinced that Bonhoeffer had been wrong in positing that the time of the innately religious being, *homo religiosus*, had passed. Such a typical figure as the human referred to in those two Latin words, who was in essence religious, had been seen by some scholars as representing *all* humans, which meant that all possessed a religious disposition and inclination. Instead, de Gruchy saw signs of intensifying religiosity in South Africa, elsewhere in Africa, and most other places. He had to say that Bonhoeffer's "prognosis that the world was moving towards a time of no religion seems to have been proved wrong, especially if we look beyond Western Europe." The South African then pointed to the many global signs that countered Bonhoeffer's vision. Like so many others, de Gruchy pondered how humanists and Christians alike might relate to a world in which the secular was as potent as Bonhoeffer saw it from his prison cell. And paradoxically, he noted, away from Europe, the religious dimension and expression appeared to be more prominent than ever.

What exactly had Robinson claimed in his section on Bonhoeffer? Among the questions with which he dealt was the one that appeared in his book title: *God*. That should be a natural topic for a book in the field of theology, but how Robinson treated it is what caused the sensation. The book was not atheistic. Instead, Robinson, picking up on his interpretation of Bonhoeffer, put God in parentheses or brackets and moved on to other themes that Bonhoeffer projected, especially "Who is Christ actually for us today?" So it is perhaps more appropriate to reach for a word like "paratheistic" or nontheistic rather than formally atheistic. In this life of the book we are interested in what scholars and others heard when the bishop spoke—he traveled widely to discourse on the plot—and what they read.

The editor of the letters and the monitor of its progress himself, Eberhard Bethge, made a succinct and helpful reference. He considered the publication a major media event, something that is not often associated with comment by Anglican bishops on earlier German Lutheran theologians in an American conjunction. Yet Robinson's little book rather quickly sold more than 350,000 copies in the Anglo-American world and, remarkably, was even translated into German and other languages. The fact that the archbishop of Canterbury saw fit to rebuke Robinson for his extreme position added to the lure of *Honest to God*. The bishop for a time made Bonhoeffer's name a household word or at least a "churchhold" word where it might otherwise have been largely ignored. Bethge pronounced a summary judgment with which most more recent scholars would concur, that Robinson picked and chose and then gave a one-sided interpretation of *Letters and Papers from Prison* to advance his own project, which had been to lead to the jostling of the church establishment and to question basic Christian doctrines. Most problematic for Bethge was the fact that Robinson's eclectic interpretation of Bonhoeffer opened the door to "creative misuse" by more radical thinkers than he.[5]

Other critics, among them one of the most noted German theologians of the time, Jürgen Moltmann, asked whether Robinson's "liberal ethical humanitarianism" provided the proper context for Bonhoeffer's Christ as "the man for others." Moltmann got to the point: "The Bishop regards the world as such, world *qua* world, as holy." That would never do for Bonhoeffer, Moltmann contended, because for him Christ was not a largely arbitrary intrusion into humanitarian talk.[6] Continental evangelical Georg Huntemann, whom we shall discuss later, further faulted Robinson for having driven away from Bonhoeffer many an evangelical who might otherwise have learned from him. His footnote is not kind, but essentially true: "Today no Bonhoeffer interpreter doubts that Robinson's *Honest to God* was a trivialization of Bonhoeffer's insights." It was now necessary, he thought, to take seriously Robinson's "shallow yet symptomatic interpretation of Bonhoeffer," only to correct it and win the evangelicals back. Building on Robinson's one-sided reading, which he thought opened to that of Hanfried Müller, Huntemann asked: "Are Bonhoeffer and Marx now to be understood as fraternal exemplary figures for a new Christo-Marxist world-and-life order?"[7]

Before turning the page from Robinson and the British scholars, one should note that almost all approvers and disapprovers agreed that Robinson had served the life of the book by forcing a focus on provocative questions posed by Bonhoeffer, whose surviving letters he could only partially and cryptically begin to answer. To advance discussion of that theme, a trip across the Atlantic to another site of Bonhoeffer study sharpens the issues. In the United States a number of professors, concurrently with Robinson's projection, went a step further into theories of secularization and evidences of the non-God perceptions and realities that came with it. The most widely read and an enduringly innovative presence on subjects like these in American theology, Harvey Cox of Harvard, drew international attention to the "secular" theme, which he found grounded or reinforced in Bonhoeffer. When Cox's *Secular City* appeared, American theologians, Protestant and Catholic alike, were showing great interest in secularity, defined in manifold ways.[8] In church and public life as they made references to Christ they would travel light when it came to church institutions, liturgy, piety, dogma, and tradition—and citing Bonhoeffer as their mentor.

Cox, in his best-selling book, had carried the secular theme far, but in a few years he drew back from his direct translation of Bonhoeffer into the secular sphere and went "back to the drawing board," as he put it. Henceforth he paid new attention to the religious, the concept and reality scorned by Karl Barth and others who influenced Bonhoeffer. With that shift or, one might better say, with his sustained dialectical view of a scene in which both the religious and the secular prospered and interacted, Cox showed himself to be reposed in historic Christianity, critically accepted. Others in the Bonhoeffer train, however, rather consistently jettisoned traditional elements.

The "Death of God" Movement

In the years marked by restless response there occurred what from the angle of mass media attention was no doubt the most sensationalistic incident in the biography of *Letters and Papers from Prison*. For a couple of years the consequent publication of a-theistic or atheistic extrapolations appeared in the United States in a period of turbulence in state and church, cultural and religious life. We are talking about "The Sixties." The brief atheism moment was confined to the activity of three or four scholars and their students and readers, but they did create a sensation, one which the press was eager to exploit and which significantly altered the course of the book's life in this, its biography.

The incident is named the "Death of God" controversy. Compare the career of the book to a journey, and this would be well described by most historians as a cul-de-sac surrounded by reverberating walls. One could enter it, survey the scene, satisfy one's curiosity, and attend to some business, but there was no way to go from there except back to the main road. It could all be dismissed as a nonevent, a dead end. Yet for what it revealed about American culture—this was not an exportable news story—and the turn that a book's influence can take, it deserves extensive notice.

Rarely in those years did the story of a theological controversy make the cover of *Time* magazine, but this one did on April 6, 1966. Its feature story referred to five living proponents of the cause, beginning with Gabriel Vahanian, who in 1961 had written a book he named *The Death of God*. It was chiefly a cultural comment that did not draw on Bonhoeffer. One rabbi, Richard Rubenstein, who at that time was writing in a "death of God" mode when he dealt with "theology after Auschwitz," was also independent of Bonhoeffer. A third professor, Paul Van Buren, used the then-dominating Anglo-American language philosophy to suggest that theological statements, which were metaphysical in background, could not be checked out empirically, and thus made no sense. He mentioned Bonhoeffer but had an agenda that would not have made a good fit in the context of German theology. The fourth, Thomas J. J. Altizer, was the most consistent asserter of a death-of-God theology, but he was less dependent on Bonhoeffer than were William Hamilton and those he directly influenced.

In his study of the letters, the Parisian Reformed theologian André Dumas took up a critique that considered the American context.[9] He affected a kind of yawn in the face of the radical theologians, reminding readers that the United States, where Hamilton and his colleagues lived, was "accustomed to a 'secular' church as well as to a state that was more or less 'religious.'" So in his eyes "a large part of the message of Bonhoeffer and his followers is thus explained by the discovery of a secularity that has been common currency in France for a long time." In effect, he was saying, "Welcome to the club, you late-comers, do your interpreting on a less naive basis." He dealt with the other best-known "death of God" theologian, William Hamilton, then of Rochester Theological Seminary, who was most consistent and concerned with Bonhoeffer's letters.[10]

Bonhoeffer himself largely escaped attention in the *Time* story. He received only a couple of brief references, perhaps because the magazine article's accent was on the American movement. One line: "During World War II, the anti-Nazi Lutheran martyr Dietrich Bonhoeffer wrote prophetically to a friend from his Berlin prison cell: 'We are proceeding toward a time of no religion at all.'" The "death of God" flap resulted largely from William Hamilton's "creative misuse" of Bonhoeffer.

When Bonhoeffer, as he did in the late letters, wrote of doing "without God," he was incautious about advancing his own new agenda. His thinking was too unfinished and abrupt, so it did not show mindfulness of what his jotted observations might mean in other contexts—such as those characteristic of tenured and thus protected academics. He was inviting both creative response and trouble. Of course, this beckoning was not yet for public consumption. He was trying out ideas on himself, Bethge, and a few friends to whom he would circulate such words. Yet it was clear that he was on the path toward more formal declarations; he even included an outline for a book on the subject, which Bethge included in *Letters and Papers from Prison.* For now, as the letters found a public, speaking and acting "without God" seemed to others, believers or not, to be strange business for theologians, since theology, in etymology and practice, has to do with words about God. There were, of course, precedents for writing radical theology at the edge of the playgrounds of scholars in the Christian tradition. Ludwig Feuerbach, in a school of thought scholars label "left-wing Hegelianism," in the nineteenth century did so. Yet such thinkers jettisoned all that went with Christian God-talk, including witness to Jesus Christ. Bonhoeffer was aware that such talk was laden with problems in his own time, but he would never have thought of departing from it.

According to Bethge's biographer, John de Gruchy, it was chiefly misinterpretations of the provocative themes that prompted Bethge to take to the lecture and conference circuit. His was not a narrow or cramping defense of friend Bonhoeffer, but a response that tried to provide some coherence among interpretations. This he did chiefly by introducing more readers and hearers to a Bonhoefferian dialectic that was lost on many literalist readers of those letters. The undialectical understandings and misunderstandings of the Bonhoeffer-inspired "death of God" theologians irritated people more than had their imputation of atheism to him. William Hamilton and Thomas J. J. Altizer were the coauthors of the sensational book of the season. The two author-editors pulled together eleven essays they had previously published, all but one of which appeared in the charged seasons between 1963 and 1965. While the authors drew on numbers of theologians and other thinkers, some of them classic and others darlings of the moment but most of them in the end forgettable and forgotten, in this life of one book I will restrict attention to the "death of God" theologians who treated Bonhoeffer as resource or detonator.

Four years before his coauthored book on Christian atheism and the death of God appeared, Hamilton had published an essay that displayed a close reading of the Bonhoeffer letters and responses to them.

He quoted from a letter written by Karl Barth on December 21, 1952, to a correspondent who was pondering Bonhoeffer's letters. Barth included an observation that became a headline for Hamilton: "The letters are a particular thorn." Such a response was a classic expression of the ambivalence the letters of Bonhoeffer frequently evoked. Barth had been miffed over some real and imagined slights to him in comments in the letters, yet he seemed in many ways enduringly to respect this representative of a younger generation. The quotation speaks to the issue and can serve as a signpost to many Bonhoeffer interpretations:

> The letters, whatever one may make of their individual sentences . . . are a particular thorn; to let them excite us can only do us all good for, unlike [Rudolf Bultmann's speciality] "demythologizing," this is unrest of a spiritual kind.
>
> What an open and rich and at the same time deep and disturbed man stands before us—somehow shaming and comforting us at the same time. That is how I also personally remember him. An aristocratic Christian, one might say, who seemed to run on ahead in the most varied dimensions. One cannot read [the letters] without having the impression that there might be something in them.[11]

It is clear that in this earlier essay Hamilton was himself being excited but was not yet formulating his "death of God" theology. He had isolated the main themes of the late and radical Bonhoeffer, including his "nonreligious interpretation of Christianity, the coming of age of the world, the need to live *etsi deus non daretur*"—"even if there were no God."

Three and four years later Hamilton was to take off from what he had written there to formulate his "theology for the death of God," identifying Bonhoeffer as someone who had done away with all forms of theism:

> Here I reflect the thought of the later Bonhoeffer more than either van Buren or Altizer wants or needs to. My Protestant has no God, has no faith in God, and affirms both the death of God and the death of all the forms of theism. Even so, he is not primarily a man of negation, for if there is a movement away from God and religion, there is the more important movement into, for, toward the world, worldly life, and the neighbor as the bearer of the worldly Jesus. We must look more carefully at these two movements: toward the world and away from religion.[12]

That comment forced Hamilton to deal with the pioneering argument started by Karl Barth, who had given his own definition of religion and then attacked what he had defined "as something like man's arrogant and grasping attempt to become God." While that definition actually placed Barth outside the scope of Hamilton's concern, the concept of religionlessness did engross both Bonhoeffer and Hamilton. Religion was associated in the latter's mind with "assorted Sabbath activities usually supported by ordained males (the moderate radicals)," but also with "any system of thought or action in which God or the gods serve as fulfiller of needs or solver of problems." So, picking up a phrase from the letters, he hailed "the breakdown of the religious *a priori* and the coming of age of man."[13]

A Hamiltonian footnote to whose substance we have already referred provides color for anyone who tries to assess the character of some theologians in this ethos. Viewing from the middle-class tenured post in a free society, Professor Hamilton reached across to the exegesis of another professor, one who is by now familiar to us, who wrote under Communism: he called Hanfried Müller's *Von der Kirche zur Welt* "the best book to date on Bonhoeffer," a judgment that has held up almost nowhere else. Hamilton lauded Müller for having connected the abolition of God with the *theologia crucis*, the "theology of the cross," but having done so without reference to the experience of the Incarnation or Resurrection of Christ. And Müller had also pleased Hamilton by connecting the theme with "a social-political optimism which, in his case of course, is derived from Marxism." There were in Hamilton's mind other directions in which to extend Bonhoeffer's reach, for example, when he also speculated that "the Negro revolution in America ... may provide a context for a similar combination of the cross and optimism."[14]

In an autobiographical essay ascribed to "Thursday's Child," his code name for Bonhoeffer, Hamilton argued that "as Western Europe turns away from Bonhoeffer as a theological mentor, we in America can welcome his fragmentary help." He cited a passage from "Thoughts on the Baptism of D. W. R.," one of the Bonhoeffer papers on the basis of which Hanfried Müller, by now quite familiar to us, argued that "atonement and redemption, regeneration, the Holy Ghost, the love of our enemies, the cross of resurrection, life in Christ and Christian discipleship—all these things have become so problematic and so remote that we hardly dare any more to speak of them." Therefore Hamilton, with his version of Bonhoeffer as mentor, wanted to be concerned with "Christian thinking, speaking, and organization," all of them now reborn in preoccupation not with God but with "our fellow men."[15]

For the twentieth anniversary of Bonhoeffer's execution, April 9, 1965, the liberal secular magazine *The Nation* asked Hamilton to write on Bonhoeffer. This he did, welcoming the chance to comment about the current theological influence that was then "still being exercised by Bonhoeffer." Hamilton presumed that the magazine's readers were not interested in the theologian as theologian. He could pass over Bonhoeffer's whole earlier career and writings in order to concentrate only on the later *Letters and Papers from Prison.* The Bonhoeffer there revealed, said the American observer, was the new person on the scene. Karl Barth and Paul Tillich, he contended, belonged to the past. Instead, "a strong case can be made that the most decisive theological influence on the younger generation of Protestants today is Dietrich Bonhoeffer." His reference to the geography, ecology, and demography of the Bonhoeffer readership, based more on intuition than on empirical observation, provided color for this chapter in the biography of the book: "Why have the fragmentary works of this young German theologian acted like a delayed time bomb in America and come into their own so recently? Bonhoeffer is not, it should be noted, an important or influential figure in West Germany or Switzerland, the traditional intellectual centers of Protestant theology. (He is important in East Germany and in Czechoslovakia, but not perhaps for the reasons we value him here.)"[16]

In Hamilton's eyes, Bonhoeffer was important "here" where cultural lag was evident in what appeared to be a slow pace of secularizing. Bonhoeffer, he noted, had instead written in a time of "the radically accelerating pace of secularization, of the increasing unimportance and powerlessness of religion, or the end of special privilege for religious men and religious institutions." Comparing him to Reinhold Niebuhr, a titan of the midcentury years, Hamilton thought Bonhoeffer and the little book of letters were "almost certainly in the process of doing for the sixties and seventies" what Niebuhr's major work had done for the two previous decades. This was the case, claimed Hamilton, for several reasons. Here was theology that left religion behind; it affirmed a nonreligious or religionless Christianity and represented a turn to the world. While Hamilton announced the death of God, sometimes God still sneaked in when Hamilton worked with the Christian tradition. So he picked up a phrase from Bonhoeffer, that "man is challenged to participate in the sufferings of God at the hands of a godless world." What the unschooled or unchurched *Nation* reader for whom Hamilton was writing would make of the apparent paradoxes in such a sentence is hard to say.

While *Honest to God* and American books on Christian atheism were best-sellers for a brief time, they also met resistance and criticism. One credible example of dismissal should suffice, since others followed similar plots. Professor Paul Lehmann, no timid theologian himself, threw up a virtual defense in the face of those he charged were misreaders of the book. He had a significant history with Bonhoeffer. As late as 1939 he had been working to arrange and offer academic posts to his German friend so he could stay in America and thus evade and avoid the deathly conflict with Hitler and Nazism. Upon the execution of Bonhoeffer in 1945 and thereafter, Lehmann felt obliged to try to keep the record straight and to reject those whose writings might lead to a misunderstanding and thus the eventual dismissal of Bonhoeffer. He read a book of one of the self-named "death of God" theologians and, seeing how that professor had run off with the concept of a "world that has come of age," called it a "careless dissemination of a half-truth," snorting that this version offered "confusion worse confounded." Lehmann and others used similar phrases to confront Robinson.[17]

Fairness demands noting that Lehmann did not say that Christian atheism was a "careless dissemination of nontruth" but of "half-truth," which means there was some truth in what was being propounded. It is true that a half-truth can rob the whole truth of its integrity and validity, but it is also important to ask what it was that Christian atheists read in Bonhoeffer that led them to respond as they did and attract an at least temporary semiserious following.

At the same time, honesty requires that anyone tracking the life of the book who reads the many interpretations of that life in the row of writings that weigh enough to make bookshelves groan will, with Lehmann, find plenty of confusion, compounded or simple, to stun the observer and inspire the critic. The confusion was not all in the minds of the interpreters. It was native to the genre and the original expression, as even editor Bethge admitted when he expressed the wish that Bonhoeffer had lived long enough to have developed and clarified his concepts. Further, Bethge thought that confusion may have resulted because he had found it necessary to burn late letters that might have explained concepts Bonhoeffer had only begun to outline. Bonhoeffer *did* write some provocative and exploratory pages. Had he not done so, his editor thought, it is quite possible that the fate of his letters and papers would have ended with them being filed in archives, explored by a few scholars, mined by some who were looking for heroes in the lore of the Nazi horror, and that would have been that.

Bethge was a bit too defensive and ready to reply. We have come to know him as a generous and mild-mannered scholar who did not always act like a censor or inhibitor. But he could not hold back any more as he read the "secular theologians" like Bishop Robinson of *Honest to God* fame or as he confronted the "death of God" writers. Where these movements referred to Bonhoeffer, Bethge complained, they misinterpreted and misunderstood his friend. Some of them, he argued, "tampered with Bonhoeffer's thought and, with an insufficient knowledge of his work, did violence to or destroyed his dialectical way of expressing himself." And he had to have little use for Hamilton as an exegete of Bonhoeffer when he heard Hamilton say, "We make a creative misuse of Bonhoeffer!" The result of the episode, he summarized, was the appearance of a set of "extremely arbitrary developments whose consequences are untrustworthy in interpreting Bonhoeffer."[18]

Few would question the fact that devotees of Robinson and Hamilton and all those who gravitated to the "honest to God" or "death of God" followings had done some vandalizing of the late letters by Bonhoeffer. They pushed all his probes to the extreme, to advance the optimistic humanism that came with their reading of Bonhoeffer. Such extreme readings provoked responses, often from people who did see that a creative misuse of the letters was advancing questions that had to be addressed, just as it inspired critiques. So ended another chapter in the biography of a book.

The Worlds of Two Strangers

Eberhard Bethge, the producer of *Letters and Papers from Prison*, had to look on in frustration as Bonhoeffer's late theology was subjected to what he called "creative misuse" by Marxists in East Germany and radicals in the Anglo-American world. By 1975 he and those of his outlook had outlasted both, so he could put perspective on them as he scanned the scene and offered his interpretation on current work that went in new paths. Some of it came from predictable and others from unanticipated directions.

The anticipated, first: "the comprehensive theological study and appraisement of his work is just beginning," Bethge asserted and was accurate when he noted: "Heinrich Ott, the only professor and head of a theology faculty who has so far devoted a full-fledged book in the German language to the study of Bonhoeffer, begins his reflections with the statement that Bonhoeffer has to be looked upon as 'one of the most hope-inspiring figures, perhaps the most hope-inspiring figure, of modern Protestantism.' The preliminary work needed to substantiate that statement has indeed gone far."[1] Ott was significant as a dealer with Bonhoeffer's legacy because he was the successor at Basel, Switzerland, to Karl Barth, who figures so frequently in discussions of Bonhoeffer. Ott was lavish in his attention to Bonhoeffer: "Our thesis is that Bonhoeffer stands at the focal point of all the important questions discussed today by theology, and that he does so in such a way that his contribution is sometimes still something to be awaited.... We believe that we can see in him the most radical and modern thinker of our time."[2]

Ott set Bonhoeffer in the context of the 1960s, especially the version of the period posed by Bishop Robinson, with whose thought he tried to be patient but which, in the end, he had to dismiss. What he had done with the theism he was attacking suggested to Ott that Robinson "*has no right whatever to quote Bonhoeffer* as an authority." He saw more promise in the unexpected turn Bonhoeffer took when he pondered the questions about belief in an ecumenical context. Ott quotes Bonhoeffer:

"What must I believe?" is the wrong question. Outdated controversies, especially the interconfessional ones; the differences between Lutheran and Reformed (and to some extent Roman Catholic) are no longer real. Of course, they can be revived with passion at any time, but they are no longer convincing. There is no proof for this. One must simply be bold enough to start from this. The only thing we can prove is that the Christian-biblical faith does not live or depend on such differences.[3]

Catholic and Evangelical Encounters

A decade later, Bethge, a custodian of the tradition, also noted how significantly the reception of Bonhoeffer among Catholics, whom I have called an "unanticipated" response group, had grown. They made up the first of two sets of commentators who were not ordinarily part of the tradition Bonhoeffer addressed. Think of them as strangers.

Ott also posed this development as having occurred after the nontheist and a-theist challenges: "Strange to say, it was Robinson's book, with its sensational publicity, and the misuse the Death-of-God theologians made of Bonhoeffer which led many Roman Catholics to explore what it was that fascinated people about Bonhoeffer's thought. I have knowledge of at least eight doctoral theses written on him by Roman Catholics."[4]

So fast have changes on the ecumenical scene occurred since 1975 that it may strike many readers as unremarkable to note the reception of Bonhoeffer among Catholic theologians, yet it was almost unprecedented in its own time. To most Protestants who were Bonhoeffer's contemporaries, Catholicism had been always "the other," the stranger if not the enemy—as also had been modern Evangelicalism.

A brief survey of the scene then and now will dramatize these two cases, which added important chapters in the biography of the book. Threescore years after *Letters and Papers from Prison* appeared, these two sets of Christians, Catholics and Evangelicals, dominate Christian news, quicken much curiosity, and are subjects of major scholarly research. Readers may recall the imagined buyer of Bonhoeffer introduced on our first pages, who thus becomes part of the book's life. The odds are quite good that, if this person were a church-going American, she would be identified as a Roman Catholic or some sort of Evangelical. She might less likely belong to a heritage called "ecumenical Protestant" in the 1960s or "mainline Protestant" today. As a matter of fact, she might also have awareness of the book and its author, who were favored in that heritage. While those who track the records will insist that Bonhoeffer today belongs to both Catholics and Evangelicals, at the time of the book's publication, most of them would have found little in his letters that grew out of or had a perceivably direct bearing on their world.

Bonhoeffer's influence, while marked, was by no means pervasive or universal in the first generation after his death. Before the Second Vatican Council (1962–1965), the Christian Church in the West had been notoriously divided. By the time the letters were published, still suspicious Catholics and Protestants had only begun to compare notes and to pay positive attention to each other. Crossing of their Christian divide was generally discouraged. East German Catholics, for instance, had other issues on their minds than noticing Protestants with favor. They were busy adjusting to change within their own communion and accommodating themselves to or fleeing from the Communist regime. They had few motives to pay attention to a dead Lutheran theologian to whose writings Christian atheists and Eastern European Communists were being drawn. Of course, one reason that Bonhoeffer received less attention from Catholics in his homeland was demographic. In 1946 Catholics represented only 12 percent of the East German population, which meant that there were 2,233,000 Catholics over against the 80 percent of the citizenry that was nominally, often *very* nominally Protestant, with its 14,963,000 adherents. It was in West Germany that the Protestant/Catholic divide was almost equal, 49.7 percent to 46.3 percent.

The biography of this book of letters, however, takes many surprising turns, few of them more representative of changes in the religious climate than was the reception and use of its message among many Roman Catholics. The pilgrimage of such a book toward Rome or its visit among Catholics would have been virtually unimaginable from the time of Martin Luther in the sixteenth century through World War II. Of course, through those centuries there were some carefully handled exchanges of scholarly texts among professors, but these were kept out of the range of a lay public. Most texts that might have been candidates for mutual study were on the Index Librorum Prohibitorum, the Catholics' screening and censoring agency, which normally forbade the circulation and reading of unapproved books, and "unapproved" was certainly the stamp on Protestant works like Bonhoeffer's.

Letters and Papers from Prison has relatively few references to Roman Catholicism. Most of them were incidental and none was polemical. How relations across faith lines within the camps and prisons could exist at all is a subject of enduring curiosity, but the letters do little to inform inquiries. The German prison and death camps incarcerated Protestants and Catholics alike. We hear, but not in these letters, of very rare circumstances in which some of them prayed together and, in one unique reported case, of a noted Protestant minister and a Catholic archbishop exchanging the consecrated bread of the Lord's Supper with each other. None of these exchanges was part of Bonhoeffer's experience. Interaction and some measure of collegiality had to wait for official encouragement by the Vatican Council. The letters themselves simply illustrate how little Catholicism had figured into the thought and action of a well-traveled and ecumenically open Protestant theologian. In a letter to his parents on May 15, 1943, he thanked them for some books they had sent him, including one he deemed congenial to someone who would meditate: "Despite all my sympathies for the *vita contemplativa* [the contemplative life], I am nevertheless not a born Trappist monk."[5] The reference is to the Cistercian order, which stipulated "enforced silence." There was not much to go on in such comment.

In a letter of November 21, 1943, Bonhoeffer wrote Eberhard Bethge of his new appreciation of church fathers, who, he now stressed, belonged not only to Catholicism, saying that "to some extent they are much more contemporaneous than the Reformers and simultaneously a basis for Protestant-catholic conversation."[6] This was an extreme kind of admission in his context. Theologians like Bonhoeffer were supposed to find nothing postbiblical to be as relevant as the Protestant reformers. Some months later Bethge, on military service in Italy, wrote about a visit to Rome, the religious art he saw there, and the audience his group had with the pope. A hint of spiritual envy was evident in Bethge's observation, "How easy it is for the Catholics now, since they can largely dispense with words" and rely chiefly on expressions such as gestures.[7] Days later the prisoner wrote back, appreciating Bethge's generally positive comment about the Vatican visit, which Bonhoeffer assumed had a different character from his own encounter a score of years earlier. He pictured the new experience as "especially inspiring and important, and added, "I assume some pig-headed Lutherans will put it down as a shameful blot on your life history, and that's precisely why I'm glad you did it."[8] Bonhoeffer also spelled out reasons why Bethge should attend the Catholic Holy Week services at particular times. His advice displayed reasonably sophisticated liturgical awareness.

In his response Bethge described how he got along in his military company through self-disciplined restraint: "each in his own fashion" plays a large part, he observed, on occasions as when colleagues compared notes and justified themselves after that papal audience. At another time Bethge reported on themes that Roman Catholic and Protestant historians treated in common, as when he chronicled "the great defection from God, from Christ." But only one reflective passage connecting his experiences with Catholicism was significant:

> I inwardly resist expressions . . . that speak of my
> "suffering." That seems like profanation. These
> things must not be dramatized. I doubt very much
> whether I'm "suffering" anymore than you or most
> other people these days. Of course, a great deal
> here is horrible, but where is it otherwise? Perhaps
> we've made too much of this question of suffering
> and been too solemn about it. I sometimes used to
> wonder how Catholics pass by such circumstances
> without even saying anything. But doesn't that
> show greater strength? Perhaps, with their history,
> they know better what suffering and martyrdom
> really are, so they remain silent about minor ha-
> rassments and hindrances.[9]

In general, such exceptional references are friendly to Catholicism, but they suggest that the view is from a distance.

Even to notice casual references today may strike some as strange, so ecumenical is the market and the audience for books like this collection of letters and papers. After the most recent half century, while no one pretends that all differences between the communions have been overcome, many biblical, liturgical, theological studies and certainly issues of social concern find a new mix of receptions among Catholics and Protestants. That was anything but the case in the time and place in which Bonhoeffer wrote. A century earlier there had been a *Kirchenkampf*, a war against the Catholic Church in Bismarck's Germany, and wounds from it were still raw. Catholics never attended Protestant seminaries and vice versa, even when the theological faculties of both were virtually under the same roof, as they were in the university town of Tübingen. Members of the dominant church bodies in Germany were not free to commune or pray with Christians across confessional lines.

Despite the paucity of references to Catholicism in the book, in the course of its life it made many friends among Catholics. The Second Vatican Council occurred between 1962 and 1965, precisely the time when what some called "the Bonhoeffer vogue" was in its prime, as East German and radical American and English theologians brought debates over the book into the academies, churches, and homes of the West.

More serious scholarship was evident in the dozens of Catholic doctoral dissertations that paid generous attention to Protestant Bonhoeffer. Whoever would note the more than tens of thousands of references on the Internet linking the words *Letters and Papers from Prison* with "Catholics" or "Catholicism" would find that a clear majority of them are generally positive and friendly. Many of these will include a phrase to the effect that "while I am Catholic and he was not," such language will be followed with discussions of Bonhoeffer's resistance to Hitler, confessions of faith, and even contributions to spiritual life across confessional boundaries.

Concern for the book's reception on Catholic soil is also of interest in a new century when the global church has become vivid to countless Christians and among those who interact positively or negatively with them on all continents. The billion Catholics vastly outnumber Protestants, Evangelicals, the Orthodox, Pentecostals, and all the other Christians. Rather than merely mentioning some of the thousands of notes and references to events, I will, here as elsewhere, take close-up views of a few representative samples.

On the very day, December 29, 2008, when I was writing this chapter about a phase in the life of the book, an admired friend, Brother Dietrich Reinhart, O.S.B., died. He was a Benedictine monk, a third-term president of St. John's University in Collegeville, Minnesota. While there were no holy wars among

Catholics and Lutherans in the Twin Cities before the council in the 1950s, back when Thomas Edward Reinhart attended St. Bridget's Elementary School there, spiritually their two camps were estranged, distant. Their priests and parents did not read books produced on the other side of the confessional divide.

Then came Pope John XXIII and the Second Vatican Council, followed by innumerable conferences, retreats, joint services of worship, shared missions, and more. A personal word: family members who joined me on a day of honors at St. John's in 2005 came to know the school's then-president, Brother Dietrich, and subsequently regularly prayed for him when his melanoma was diagnosed. One thing we had never discussed during the months of vigil was his first name. "Reinhart" is a sufficiently German name to attract "Dietrich" as a surname. Only in his obituary did we learn that this Catholic monk, upon making his vows and being asked to choose a monastic name, "asked for the name of Dietrich in honor of Dietrich Bonhoeffer, the great German Lutheran theologian who was a participant in the resistance movement against Nazism." He was honoring the author of *Letters and Papers from Prison*.

A terse symbolic seal on the Catholic reception of the book, at least in America, is the inclusion of a hymn by Bonhoeffer in numbers of hymnals and choir books widely used in Catholic worship. This occurred because Bethge had included a poem by Bonhoeffer, which was condensed and redrafted by Fred Pratt

Green. In the hymnals it was transformed from "Powers of Good" in *Letters and Papers from Prison* to the hymn "By Gracious Powers." The original lines were written during the author's last months and appeared in the book between two virtual farewell letters dated December 28, 1944, and January 17, 1945, and sent to Bonhoeffer's parents. That last letter included directions to his parents to "give away whatever anyone might need, without giving it a second thought."[10] Bethge, by saving the poem, gave to the church one of the great modern hymns, and some Catholics who treasure such writings have adopted it.

For many Catholics, the question of sainthood is more attractive than it is for Protestants. Some Catholics have begun to debate whether Protestants like Martin Luther King, Jr., should be canonized. On the short list of other possible candidates is Bonhoeffer, for his death in resistance to Nazism. Catholic iconographers who depict near-contemporary figures offer icon-cards with the name and face of Bonhoeffer on them. He is occasionally referred to, though, of course, not invoked, in prayers, where he is cited as an exemplar. In his letters Bonhoeffer recalled a conversation he had held in America with Jean Lasserre, a French pastor who said he would like to become a saint. To this recall Bonhoeffer added a parenthesis, "(and I think it's possible that he did become one)." But the German disagreed with the French friend, because he wanted and needed "faith," not "sainthood," to help him live completely in this world.[11]

Still, *Letters and Papers from Prison* comes up occasionally in discussions as to whether the category of "saint" could apply to Bonhoeffer. On first hearing of the discussion, an informed reader may wonder why the name of a notable Protestant should come up at all in discussions of sainthood. In the popular imagination, "postbiblical" saints are a Catholic preoccupation. True, many Lutheran churches in America are named after "St. Paul" and "St. Luke" and, on very rare occasions "St. Mary" or "St. Mary Magdalene," but, after their biblical canon was virtually closed, Protestants also closed the door on talk about new saints. They spoke of abuses against which Martin Luther and the other Protestant originators rebelled. Saints had been and often still were invoked in ways they regarded as superstitious. Just as often, instead of providing access to God when someone was praying, the mention and idea of saints, critics thought, blocked passage. They quoted a biblical reference to the effect that there was only one mediator between God and the human: Jesus Christ. To invoke others went against the biblical witness.

True, in some Protestant churches, including the Lutheran, and no doubt in the Bonhoeffer experience, certain cherished saints from the Catholic calendar lived on, especially in church names. There were and are Lutheran churches, especially in Europe, named St. Barbara, St. Lawrence, or St. Martin. In the United States, Scandinavian immigrants on occasion brought along the names of cherished churches and transplanted them as St. Olaf, St. Lucie, St. Ansgar, and more. But it is not part of evangelical Protestant understandings to appeal to them, invoke them, or evoke their continued work before the throne of God on behalf of petitioners or those seeking perfection. If this is true of saints who were appealed to through the centuries, it is certainly true of near-contemporaries. Protestants have no official way of canonizing saints in any case, but Catholicism does. So it would be very interesting to learn of any people who died during the century past appealing to Catholics as candidates for sainthood if they were not Catholics themselves. In his lively book *Making Saints,* Kenneth Woodward told of some Lutherans who approached Catholic "saint-makers" and wondered whether they could advance the cause of Dietrich Bonhoeffer. They were told that, admired though Bonhoeffer was among Catholics, it would have been a distortion of the concept of canonization in Catholicism to think of this Protestant in that context. In effect: go home, Lutherans, think through the meanings of sainthood, and do your own canonization of people like Bonhoeffer, whom Lutherans revered, even as did veteran saint-watcher Woodward.[12]

It *is* very telling, then, to see Dietrich Bonhoeffer taken seriously when one of the most noted Catholic commentators on sainthood and saints proposed him as a case study. Lawrence S. Cunningham, a no-nonsense scholar who deals with spiritual traditions, has important things to say on this subject. He speaks of Mother Teresa of Calcutta and Thomas Merton, a Cistercian monk of world renown, as the best cases. Then—surprise!—the third in number of mentions is Dietrich Bonhoeffer. Significantly, Cunningham, who has no "saint-making" power, talks about Bonhoeffer when he speaks in the book-length comment on *The Meaning of Saints*, since for him Bonhoeffer exemplifies so much in the category of "heroic sanctity." He has to define a saint and does: "A saint is a person so grasped by a religious vision that it becomes central to his or her life in a way that radically changes the person and leads others to glimpse the value of that vision." That "being grasped" is a necessary but, of course, not sufficient element in the discussion of sanctity on heroic levels.[13]

Let lay Catholics vote, Cunningham says, and one finds some non-Catholics and even some non-Christians on the roster of candidates. Among these are the Hindu Mohandas Gandhi, the unorthodox Christian Albert Schweitzer, and then Bonhoeffer. "What strikes one about a Dietrich Bonhoeffer is not that he died at the hands of the Gestapo but that he reflected, prayed, wrote, counseled, and lived under the extreme circumstance of a Gestapo regime." The Christian response within extremity of circumstance matters for him.

Cunningham would not know of Bonhoeffer's response to those circumstances, aside from a few observations by fellow prisoners, were it not for *Letters and Papers from Prison*. "The posthumous publication of his *Letters and Papers from Prison* permitted us to see a person who was not merely heroic but saintly. It was only because those papers were saved that we could glimpse a spiritual life that would have meaning for us being developed. The hidden witness of his religious fidelity became apparent almost fortuitously."

Cunningham's chapter is fairly brief, but on the extended literary and more formal theological level there are many more Catholic works, three of which I will note. The first, by Parisian Jesuit René Marlé, was intended as a general introduction to Bonhoeffer, and explicit references to Catholic emphases and viewpoints were slight. In the case of his book, it is worthy of note that a Jesuit in 1967, soon after the Vatican Council, could deal with the substance of a Protestant thinker's writings without finding it necessary or even important to shuttle back and forth with emphasis on Catholic particularities. The priest had earlier specialized in the study of modern Protestants like Rudolf Bultmann. Marlé confessed that he first came to study Bonhoeffer on the basis of *Letters and Papers from Prison*, which he had read ten years earlier, as an antidote to "the impoverishing influence of Bultmann."[14]

Bonhoeffer's partly radical reputation, he reported, had spread by then. Some years after his first reading, the priest was asked by a colleague whether he had heard of Bonhoeffer, "who was said to be more 'frightening' than Bultmann," and to have gone "much further" in watering down the Christian faith. Marlé sputtered: "I could hardly contain my astonishment, and indeed indignation, at what seemed to me so serious a misconception." Chalk up two more motivations among those who were touched by the life of this book: to release indignation and to set a record straight. His book, published in French as *Dietrich Bonhoeffer, Témoin de Jésus-Christ parmi ses frères*, is largely an exposition of the life work but in the last chapter he did write, as well he might be expected to, of the "disturbing vision" encountered there. After noting that "Bonhoeffer is known by his letters from prison, more than by any of the other books we have discussed up to now," the Jesuit was refreshingly honest: "I am quite sure that, *as they are expressed*, Bonhoeffer's ideas are not merely disturbing, but actually dangerous." The fact that Marxist theologian Müller found the book so attractive and unusual was part of what caused the disturbance. Thus: "On his scholarly work on Bonhoeffer, *Von der Kirche zur Welt* (From the Church to the World), the east German theologian, Müller, uses [the disturbing and dangerous words] to prove that, in the mind of the 'final,' in other words of the only genuine, Bonhoeffer, the Church can be truly fulfilled only by participating in the construction of socialism." Marlé was himself further disturbed that "some rash people have made Bonhoeffer their authority by putting forward an attack on traditional Christianity which practically amounts to destroying it altogether." Bonhoeffer, he said, was aware of dangers inherent in "any study of obviously incomplete and one-sided reflexions of this kind, developed solely from a critical point of view."[15]

After writing in appreciation of Bonhoeffer's life of prayer and devotion, as these would appeal to a Catholic sensibility, Marlé took up those ideas that *as they are expressed* were "not merely disturbing, but actually dangerous." The proof of that danger was obvious in the context that is relevant here, in the way they have been used for Communist interpretations by Hanfried Müller and others. Marlé noted how often Bonhoeffer himself regarded his ideas as being on the edge, risky, half-formed, easily misused, and how often the prisoner half worked out his thoughts by using question marks. Yet the Catholic sought and found in the Lutheran a great supply of witnesses to the "vertical" dimensions of Christian life, including the hope of resurrection.

It was on the last two pages that the confessional issue finally came up:

> It is true that Bonhoeffer appreciated some of the values closely linked with the Catholic tradition: not only the sense of a visible Church and the blessings of life in community, but also the sense of a faith rooted in the "penultimate" realities of nature and history. Yet the Church to which he remained passionately attached through his life was primarily the Protestant Church, which meant for him a Church striving to live by the gospel alone.... Though we do not necessarily subscribe

to his picture of our Church, we have much to gain by acting upon his reminders and warnings. . . .

And the encounter we can still have with Bonhoeffer in his writings seems to me one which should be of first priority for us all.[16]

Marlé, who thought that dialogue with Bonhoeffer ought to stress the sacramentality that Catholics recognized and which the priest also glimpsed in Bonhoeffer, accented some often neglected features of the letters. Rather than dive right into the controversies over the "world that has come of age," "religionless Christianity," and Christ as "the man for others," he celebrated what Bethge found in him, a person who "knew that a man could enjoy the beauty of this world, while being ready to sacrifice it: [whether] the fruits of the earth, the warmth of the sun, friendships, fun, or wit. He was greatly drawn to people who could turn a meal into something special. He taught others how to celebrate a festivity. He could sacrifice all these things, yet even when sacrificing them, he loved to show others how to make the most of the beauties of the world."[17]

What impresses a person who comes to the scene decades later to track the biography of a book as it lands on Catholic soil and in Catholic libraries is the fact that very seldom must an interpreter like Marlé fall back on extensive distinctively Roman Catholic interests and interpretations to address his own inquiries and concerns. He recognized that though Bonhoeffer wrote on ecumenism from a Protestant viewpoint, he was displaying an ecumenical spirit. He also noticed that Catholic interpreters during and after the time of the ecumenical breakthrough in the Vatican Council found that Bonhoeffer had shifted the issues to points where Catholics and Protestants shared common fears and hopes—and resources. Bonhoeffer still remained "other" to Catholics, but his example and writings had done much to effect some bridging.

The other major example of Catholic reckoning with the life of this book is more revealing. Written between 1966 and 1969 and published in a revised and now standard edition in 1971 by a Catholic professor from Munich, Ernst Feil, it is *The Theology of Dietrich Bonhoeffer*. The author was a favorite of Eberhard Bethge and remains one of the most profound and sensitive interpreters of Bonhoeffer. What impressed me as I read it was both how Catholic his book is and how few explicit references to Roman Catholicism are in it. This is so because Feil captured Bonhoeffer writing how the drastically changed context of theology and faith in "the world that has come of age" not only had served to make many levels of Lutheran-Reformed conflict obsolete, but that the same was true of Protestant and Catholic separatenesses. Not that Bonhoeffer did not take theological differences seriously. He simply found that a new situation had led to the new agenda, which Catholics and non-Catholics in an ecumenical era mutually approached.[18]

Feil made little of his own Catholic worldview in introducing the book that was being translated. His emphasis was clear in the first line: "Christ and the world come of age—this is the theme of Bonhoeffer's life and theology." While at home with the vast Bonhoeffer literature, he did what we are doing in this biography of a book, as he sought "to explain Bonhoeffer's view of Christian faith lived in a religionless world." Well aware that the book was traveling and finding new homes, he announced at once: "The more significant [Bonhoeffer] and his work become in countries whose political situations challenge Christian faith in a special way, the more serious must be the effort to discern Bonhoeffer's real intention." As a Catholic, Feil did look for a special angle and found it in its choice of focus and subject matter: "The subject of the world has attracted increasing attention in recent theology. Hitherto the world was not really a matter for systematic reflection in Roman Catholic theology, since all that was necessary had been said in the doctrine of creation."[19]

Also at once he threw himself into the ongoing controversy over the Marxist interpretation by setting his view in polar opposition to that of Müller and his colleagues. Müller had claimed to see that the letters represented a "qualitative leap" from Bonhoeffer's earlier work, while the Catholic Feil stressed continuity, thus taking sides in the debate between two major camps of interpreters of the book: one group argued that the letters of 1944 on "religionless Christianity" represented a radical breach as they made up what we may call the "discontinuity" faction among interpreters. They obscured and left behind Bonhoeffer's writings from the previous score of years. Feil based part of his argument favoring continuity on the Catholic theology in which he had been schooled, though he wanted to transcend what he called "denominational" boundaries.

> The point of departure in this study of Bonhoeffer is the Catholic understanding of faith, but only one of several possibilities of reflection arising from that understanding is to be considered. With regard to Bonhoeffer's theological consideration of the world, it is impossible to sustain denominational differences (as if Bonhoeffer's theology of the world were a specifically Protestant one to which a specifically Catholic response could be given.) Theological interpretations of Christian life in the world differ widely but those distinctions are not always caused by differences between denominations. They can also be quite in agreement without thereby suggesting that denominational differences have been overcome.[20]

Then came this polemical differentiating paragraph, which he footnoted with the names of Catholic William Kuhns and Lutheran Werner Elert:

> This denominational question brings into focus the necessity for readers of Bonhoeffer to accept the man as he understood himself and as he lived,

namely as a Protestant Christian and theologian. It is illegitimate for Catholics to claim him directly for their cause; but it is equally wrong for Protestants to reject Bonhoeffer, with the argument that he "Romanizes" the Protestant religion, and thus to dispense with the imperative of truly recognizing Bonhoeffer's denominational position.

Feil insisted on what appears to be obvious, though it was often overlooked at first by some interpreters, which was that Bonhoeffer's approach was Christological. Feil offered one of the best summaries of Christology in the prison letters, and we will return to his treatment at the end of this book. Christology, Feil repeatedly stressed, was the guiding principle, focus, and perspective for Bonhoeffer's "theological understanding of the world." As already noticed but deserving of emphasis: he was sure that Müller was most wrong when he spoke of "qualitative leaps" in Bonhoeffer, as revealed in his late letters.[21] Intending to deal with Bonhoeffer comprehensively, Feil made use of each stage of Bonhoeffer's writing. Since I am writing the biography of a book, with the conceit that only this book of all the prisoner's writings is available to the reader in whose library it is deposited in splendid isolation, I cannot retrace the earlier steps, stages, and writing but will focus on the summary positions of scholars like Feil. The earlier writings do foreshadow much that is in *Letters and Papers from Prison*.

To the present point: all along, Bonhoeffer wanted to be sure that nothing he wrote would be read as a witness against Roman Catholicism. He thought that only the doctrine of justification by faith really separated the two communions, adding that he was concerned not with the terms "Protestant" and "Catholic" but with the word of God. These were shocking words in the 1940s, since that there was a permanent breach was the common assumption in both communions.

Superintendent Julius Rieger, Berlin-born pastor of the German Lutheran St. Georges Church in London in 1964, remembered how Bonhoeffer once mentioned casually that in a certain church in Rome, "I forget which, he had felt sorely tempted to become a Roman Catholic." Given Bonhoeffer's interests in pre-Reformation Christian thought, liturgy and liturgical renewal, and some features of Catholic philosophy, some pecksniffy German Lutherans suspected that he would turn Catholic. He was to them a "Romanizer," a "Catholicizer." Feil, aware of this, offered an astute observation about accents discernable in the letters from prison: "Precisely because he may very well have been tempted to convert to Roman Catholicism, but did not do so, Bonhoeffer must be taken ever more seriously as a Protestant Christian and theologian and, thus, be spared the dubious charge of being a 'Catholicizer.'"[22] Catholicism thus remained an "other" to prisoner Bonhoeffer, but in the prison letters and earlier, he had worked to bridge between communions.

The Other Stranger: Evangelicalism

Since the publication of the letters, on a global scale the Christian and other publics have become aware of a second giant "other," as Catholicism had been for almost half a millennium, and this new cohort in some sectors of Christianity prospered even more than did Catholicism. Call it, as most people have come to do, Evangelicalism. In Europe the number of those in the Protestant churches of the sort with which Bonhoeffer was most familiar declined in "the world that has come of age." There was also more moderate decline in North America, even as the number was expanding in selective Asian and African examples. However, the years since his book took on a life of its own have seen dramatic rises in what came to be called Evangelical, Fundamentalist, and Pentecostal Christian—often described as Conservative—cohorts. While roughly one-third of world population was named Christian in 2000, as it had been in 1900, within that fraction these Catholic and Evangelical sectors prospered globally—Western Europe partly aside—against secularizing trends.

It is rather easy to report on Catholic responses, since definitions of who is Roman Catholic and who is not are decisive. The other story is more difficult to tell, since it deals with the relative sprawl of conservative Protestantism, and especially Evangelicalism, in its Protean shapes. For one thing, "Evangelical," the name that won out in translation in more cultures than not, has meant many different things in those various environments. In the eyes of some, informed by American Protestant history, the Fundamentalist connections to and the connotations of the term prevail. Fundamentalists for almost a century have come to represent a worldwide multi- and nondenominational front of reactors to modernity, even if they were most skilled among the churches at employing the physical instruments of modernity such as radio, television, and the Internet to gather their groups and spread their message. Notably but not surprisingly, *Letters and Papers from Prison* found no place to rest among staunch Fundamentalists who, if they were aware of Bonhoeffer at all, wrote him off completely. Most of them had been denominational separatists, mingling only with their own kind, and in every respect Bonhoeffer was an outsider. All they had to know about his book is that it bore no evidence of their own insistent belief in the inerrancy of the Bible or in biblical interpretations they called "literal."

Still restricting this tracing of a term to America, historians record that more moderate Evangelicals who spun off from Fundamentalism or who perpetuated the patterns of nineteenth-century non-Fundamentalist Evangelicalism had at least a potential case for making selective use of Bonhoeffer. It must be said, however, that their employment of Bonhoefferian themes and their devotion to him as exemplar and hero were limited largely to his works that antedate his imprisonment. Always uneasy about his approach to biblical authority, seeing it as firm and principled but not regarding the Bible as inerrant, such Evangelicals could not embrace the theologian even where they admired some aspects of his life and witness. Most have been dismissive of the letter-writer from prison who could speak of a "world that has come of age," "religionless Christianity," acting as if there were no God, and seeing Jesus Christ as "the man for others." His book was simply unacceptable among them.

The term "Evangelical" needs some explanation in context. In Germany it often served as an equivalent to Protestant, particularly Lutheran but also often Reformed churches. It was invented in the sixteenth century, especially by those who did not want the Protestant Reformation narrowed to words like "Lutheran" or "Reformed." In the state-supported churches of Central and Western Europe it came to be part of the official name in various nations or territories. The basic design was to differentiate its churches from the Roman Catholic. This usage is quite different from what Evangelicalism connotes in the United States. For convenience's sake we can turn for an authoritative digest by the most influential historian of American Fundamentalism and its moderate offspring, George Marsden. He identified five defining characteristics: "the Reformation doctrine of the final authority of Scriptures, (2) the real, historical character of God's saving work, (3) eternal salvation only through personal trust in Christ, (4) the importance of evangelism and missions, and (5) the importance of a spiritually transformed life."[23]

Often the term can be used in relaxed ways associated with the official and established Protestant churches. However, in times of stress and doctrinal controversy, it is the more conservative party that adopts and applauds the name. Such parties link spiritually and often strategically with counterparts around the world. The kind of Evangelicalism that is of interest here is of the more partisan and often reactionary type. In 1960 it was estimated that 50 million Evangelical Christians flourished in the West and 25 million elsewhere. Today there are an estimated 75 million in the West and 325 million in the rest of the world. Many, if not most, in that number are Pentecostal, for whom Bonhoeffer is ordinarily neither here nor there, and where visions of a "world that has come of age" and "religionless Christianity" would not be comprehensible or welcome.

The attitude of American Evangelicals to Bonhoeffer is revealing both for what it tells about their movement and because it illustrates the amplitude of Bonhoeffer's vision and the many ways his probing final letters are being read in many contexts. The literature on the American subject, much of it in periodicals, is vast. One of the more helpful means of access to it is in the survey work of Stephen B. Haynes, long a bibliographer and trend-spotter on this front. He exposed the American Evangelical scene to public view and framed discourse on the topic through a paper he presented at the Tenth International Bonhoeffer Congress in Prague in 2008. He later published it as "The American Evangelical Love Affair with Dietrich Bonhoeffer."[24]

Love may be too strong a word; better to speak of favorable attention being paid. Haynes pointed out that polled readers of *Christian History*, partner publication of the flagship Evangelical journal *Christianity Today*, named Bonhoeffer the "highest ranked theologian" of the century. In all four categories of popularity and influence he rated in the top ten, along with only Billy Graham, C. S. Lewis, Mother Teresa, and Martin Luther King, Jr.[25]

Haynes chronicled the way the engagement has been pursued, as Evangelicals saw Bonhoeffer to be a "Christian hero, cultural warrior, internal critic, and ecclesiological guide." Militant Evangelicals such as Charles Colson, Pat Robertson, and James Dobson summoned the ghost of Bonhoeffer to their side for battles they were waging. Critical Evangelicals such as David Gushee and Glen Stassen favorably all but described him as a liberation theologian, while leaders of a new movement, "The Emerging Church," cited him as a pioneer on the ecclesiological front.[26]

So far, so good—but *only* so far. Haynes also found that Evangelicals were ambiguous about Bonhoeffer when it came to the interpretation of his late prison letters. Few could repudiate Bonhoeffer on the basis of negative judgments concerning these, but knowledge of them also led many to be cautious and critical.

So it was that, as Haynes noted, "in fact, there is no post-Reformation theologian whose words carry more clout among American evangelicals" than he, yet from the beginnings of their love affair, during the time radical theologians were preempting him, some opposed him bitterly. Therefore, "four decades after the death-of-God movement faded into theological oblivion," Haynes noted, "there is still a great deal of evangelical ambivalence toward the letters and papers penned by this martyr months before his execution. How can this be explained?"

Simply: *Letters and Papers from Prison.*

Let Haynes provide a context to enhance the drama:

[I]t appears that American evangelicals are still reluctant to embrace the Bonhoeffer of *Letters and Papers from Prison*, displaying a reserve that is not evident in the mainstream of American Christianity. In 2000, for instance, when HarperCollins named the best spiritual books of the twentieth century, *Letters and Papers from Prison* was number two (just behind *Black Elk Speaks*[!]). Yet as evangelical publications released lists of the best religious books around the same time, *Letters and Papers from Prison* was never mentioned.[27]

Cogently, I believe, Haynes asked his own question and then began to answer it: "How do we explain this?" First, the book is not devotional or helpful for preaching, as others in Bonhoeffer's corpus are. Second, and perhaps more important: many Evangelicals are suspicious about Bonhoeffer's orthodoxy, since he seems too much at home with the suspect neo-orthodox writers, people like Karl Barth, Rudolph Bultmann, and Paul Tillich. Tendencies toward suspect neo-orthodoxy show up most in *Letters and Papers from Prison*. Some Evangelical writers, not willing to see Bonhoeffer's reputation suffer, find ways to make his late writings sound rather orthodox, if on different grounds than Catholics and ecumenical Protestants do. But "more often," Haynes notes, "evangelicals simply ignore the prison letters or pass over their theological significance." When they cannot ignore Bonhoeffer at this point, they stress the positive and majority themes in the letters: Bonhoeffer's prison experience, including "his maintenance of spiritual discipline, his ministry to other prisoners, and his faithfulness unto death." They "remain unimpressed by prescient theological ruminations, even those as profound as Bonhoeffer's." Haynes's judgment is born out in the Evangelical textual evidence. The most detailed example of this is *Bonhoeffer: Pastor, Martyr, Prophet, Spy*. Best-selling author Eric Metaxas wrote from an emphatically Evangelical point of view, avoiding or downplaying the radical questioning and proposals by Bonhoeffer in his late letters.[28]

Since Evangelicals provide a large market for books, one might slightly wryly note that booksellers might be satisfied with the bargain that comes with ambivalence: they can prosper selling everything by and about

Bonhoeffer except the book whose life we are tracing, *Letters and Papers from Prison*. That would also be a cynical reading. Clearly, many Evangelicals are on the move from frozen positions they held or stereotypes they suffered, and Bonhoeffer, always an inspirer and often an enigma, will continue to be a challenge most will welcome.

Less familiar to readers in the English-speaking world are the Evangelicals in Europe, and even less familiar is the attention many have paid to Bonhoeffer, especially when they had to wrestle with the controversial late letters. Yet attention to their writings not only opens the view to Evangelical diversity in Europe but also suggests how they—like so many others, it must be said—make use of Bonhoeffer to satisfy their interests. To illustrate this, we will take a full-length view of one very expressive figure and his writings.

A European Evangelical Case Study

The choice is the revisionist *The Other Bonhoeffer*, by self-described Evangelical Georg Huntemann. In the spring of 1989 this Reformed professor, then in Basel, Switzerland, published a book that treated Bonhoeffer synoptically and found enough in *Letters and Papers from Prison* to develop points he fostered. A convert from a self-described radical past, he had become a crusader for many Evangelical causes and a fierce polemicist against many forces that to him represented lethal challenges to Christianity and culture. He described his context among Evangelicals:

> They are called "evangelicals," those Bible-believing, reformational (sometimes more pietistic), revivalist Christians—Christians who hold to conservative values and therefore live in basic opposition to their times. They are irritated when they hear the name "Bonhoeffer." They generally do not know what to make of the man who is perhaps the most widely read German-speaking theologian in the twentieth century. To be sure, the prayers from *Letters and Papers from Prison* often hang in church foyers and prayer rooms, framed or as posters. There is even a very famous revivalist hymn that contains a prayer from Bonhoeffer. A sentence of two from *The Cost of Discipleship* is appreciatively accepted.[29]

A few of his causes are easily summarized and cataloged. Thus he set out:

- To listen to and then radically reject all interpretations of the letters from the Left, symbolized and provoked by Hanfried Müller/s Marxist approach;
- To defend Bonhoeffer from those who thought he was assaulting the patriarchal and aristocratic ethos of the old order in prewar Germany;
- To try to make the case that that old order was worth reconstructing on renewed bases;

- To criticize most things labeled as "modern" or "modernist";
- Vehemently to denounce feminism in church and society, seeing it as a typical but most destructive cultural feature; he could even connect feminism and attacks on fatherhood with the Hitlerism that Bonhoeffer opposed;
- To support order.

If Bishop Robinson and Hanfried Müller could find texts in Bonhoeffer to confirm what they stood for, so could Huntemann. He carried a burden: the European Evangelicals he addressed had largely repudiated Bonhoeffer by the time he was writing. However, he found satisfying texts in Bonhoeffer's letters that were critical of major Protestant liberal theologians, figures whom Huntemann constantly criticized. In matters of state, his Bonhoeffer not only opposed Hitler but did so, argued Huntemann, in part to defend the traditional order, another of his main interests.

While much of Evangelicalism in the Northern Hemisphere was religiously conservative, its representatives also were often attracted to economic and politically conservative positions and alignments. Huntemann was anything but an exception. He went so far as to praise Bonhoeffer for being bourgeois, a judgment that some modern liberal theologians who read the letters considered a liability of the man they favored. He even saw Bonhoeffer as a potential rescuer of a kind of Christian aristocracy. Liberals who had picked liberal themes out of Bonhoeffer's prison letters had no place for such contentions. In a context and with terms latter-day Americans would understand, Huntemann was "firming up his base," though in slightly unconventional terms.

Quite typically for the times when *Letters and Papers from Prison* appeared, Huntemann set out to counter feminism, which was controversial in European Protestantism, and especially in its Evangelical wings. The staunch professor was both "preaching to the choir" and trying to show the door to others whom he considered to be fatuous, ideological, or heretical. He stated his own case:

> It has occurred to me that Bonhoeffer's struggle against National Socialist ideology can readily be carried over to our day. The patriarchal figure Bonhoeffer, for whom the assigned place of the woman was the household of her husband and to whom it was crucial that the wife be subject to the husband, this Bonhoeffer, who fought for an ethos "from above" and for a governmental authority "by God's grace"—this Bonhoeffer was no comrade of the Nazis nor fitting contemporary of these times. Furthermore—and this is a very important aspect of this book for me—all of the anti-Christian elements of the Nazi period continue to be at work precisely among those who count themselves, often with such careless disregard of history, part of the progressive or left-wing

scene. This is the case in spite of the fact that these anti-Christian elements appear in a different conceptual raiment than the garments they wore during National Socialism. The more or less matriarchal, socially utopian, and merely selectively biblical theology in Germany (and not only in Germany) cannot appeal to Bonhoeffer to support its claim. Moreover, it stands in complete contradiction to that which Bonhoeffer wanted to accomplish through his thought and life.[30]

Whether to trust such a witness to describe what makes up polite and kind writing, which Huntemann said he favored, is questionable among those stunned by such a blast. Lingering over the passage is not an idle diversion for readers, however, because it so well represents, though (I hope) in hyperbolic form, a polemic against feminism, which helps explain why apologists for *Letters and Papers from Prison* often encounter suspicion from feminists and—to borrow a Huntemann-style locution—"not only from feminists."

A larger context of his Evangelical antifeminism, which we shall note, appeared in Huntemann's concern over one Bonhoeffer text. The editor had included it as "Thoughts on the Day of the Baptism of Dietrich Wilhelm Rüdiger Bethge." Bonhoeffer wrote portentously: "We may have to face events and changes which run counter to our rights and wishes." That line worried Huntemann, who saw it as "an anticipation of anti-Fascist, democratic, social upheaval," the kind

Müller and his East German compatriots were celebrating. Huntemann countered them by saying that here Bonhoeffer was "thinking not only of the social position of the individual, but also of the social position of the church, as one sees in [his remark in the book] . . . that 'the old country parsonage and the old town villa will belong to a vanished world.'"[31]

In many ways, Huntemann conceived of his rather defensive book as a kind of rescue mission of Bonhoeffer, and in doing so he made a contribution to the biography of the book. As he saw it, not without reason, some liberal, secular-minded, and even atheistic sorts had seized on feminist themes. They could contribute to the cause of rendering guilt by association. By taking the "world coming of age" sayings out of context and thus doing violence to the life work of Bonhoeffer, they were threatening the theological scaffold on which that life work had been built. Just as with actual dealings with a human person, who is viewed differently depending upon the experience of the viewer, so the biography of a book was being approached by responders who often contradicted each other.

There were good reasons, we have seen, for progressives and radicals to have seized the book for their purposes, since some of the more provocative visionary pages of the letters did inspire those who wished to jettison many traditional understandings of the faith. They found it advantageous to use the honored name of a theologian who stood steadfastly against the Nazi forces, even unto death. However, there were also good reasons, as Huntemann knew, for conservatives to have picked up the book and found some of their theology reinforced—particularly, the devotion by Bonhoeffer to Jesus Christ, consistent and often overlooked by heedless or reactionary conservative Christians.

No doubt there was some risk in all this for Huntemann, because by the 1980s, thanks to international controversies over the book, the conservative Protestant leadership had become well aware of the radical interpretations of Bonhoeffer, and a friendly advocate, if he made even a small misstep, could lose reputation in the rather close-knit company of Evangelical theologians on both sides of the Atlantic. To those familiar with the arguments over Bonhoeffer, it is tempting to say that Huntemann had to do some gerrymandering with the text, putting special spins on it, and had to be ingenious in inventing ways to interpret the book. To anticipate the outcome: he conceived of an approach using a concept rarely associated with Bonhoeffer, modern mainstream theologians, or, for that matter, much in the German Evangelical traditions. He called it Christ-mysticism.

For all that, Huntemann's case was troubling, though for reasons other than those that were associated with the Marxist or Christian-atheist interpretations that were momentarily in vogue: Huntemann stated the conservative Evangelicals' case in the form of questions he knew were being posed by those who were skeptical about treating the author of the letters positively. Thus, he heard them asking many questions, such as: Didn't Bonhoeffer dirty himself with politics more than a Christian should? Didn't he say the wrong things about "the powerlessness of God," about humans "coming of age," and then living without "the God hypothesis"? Wasn't he too sure that humans now could face God's "otherworldliness" in the midst of this world? Hadn't he even written that the most radical alternative to "Bible-believers," Rudolf Bultmann, was not radical enough? Huntemann counted heads of theologians who nodded and murmured agreement when the idea of Bonhoeffer's heterodoxy came up.

To add spice and drama, he referred to a celebrated cause of the day in the form of a camp of confessional and creedal church pastors who called their movement "No Other Gospel." They decided that Bonhoeffer represented such an "other" to the Christian gospel to which they were devoted. The moment postwar progressivism began to flourish in West Germany, this group filled halls and auditoriums to counter it. "Since that time," Huntemann wrote, "Bonhoeffer has been viewed by most German evangelicals exclusively in the dark shadow of postwar modernism." Few epithets carried more burden of stigma than that in the decades after the war, as German Protestants and their theological neighbors were trying to reassemble their forces. They did not need Bonhoeffer for that task, nor could they naturally welcome his advocacy. Huntemann wanted to clear a space for himself, since he wanted to be an effective advocate, and he used this book to further the cause.

For an Evangelical, such clearing meant confessing his sins. Deviating from orthodoxy was a virtual Deadly Sin. After examining himself, as a sinner would, Huntemann reported that his reading of the Bonhoeffer letters, which began in 1951, had led him to make a variety of responses. "I was stirred by the realism and the dynamic totality of his theology," he wrote, but when the modernists engaged in what one scholar called "creative abuse" of the theologian, he wrote that he had become "irritated and disconcerted by Bonhoeffer" and even wrote some things against Bonhoeffer. Whereupon, "a man from Stuttgart by the name of Rainer Mayer" read the polemical writings and—note the reputation for rudeness and unkindness of theologians in this company—it was "a very surprising letter . . . surprising because it was unusually polite and kind for a letter from a theologian." Mayer, in responding, sent along some books he had written on Bonhoeffer. These were convincing and brought about Huntemann's eventual change of heart. Just as Evangelicals like to confess, they also like to see the fruits of repentance. In this case, it was a call to reread Bonhoeffer, the penitent wrote, "and the result is this book."

What we have just read is a comparison that uses the word "precisely" to equate Christian feminists and those Huntemann locates in the camp of "progressive" and "left-wing" scenes. Bonhoeffer, he found, had been "polite" and "kind" in making his case. Just as the radical modernists were overly sure of what Bonhoeffer would have stood for had he survived, so it is risky to project or guess how he would have dealt with Christian, including much Evangelical, feminism. True, decades later there are still fierce Protestant holdouts against the ordination of women, for example, in Latvian Lutheranism and the Southern Baptist Convention in the United States. Yet, that tendency aside, as women came to be the best-selling Evangelical authors, heads of televised evangelistic empires, and leaders in political and economic realms, the non-Utopian, non-left-wing progressives among Evangelical women can be embarrassed three or four generations later by some of Bonhoeffer's views, as they appear also in *Letters and Papers from Prison.*

Huntemann claimed simply that "Bonhoeffer was conservative" as an ethicist, because he "advocated rule and order on the basis of revelation." On the key Evangelical theological point, he appeared to be sufficiently polemical to take a mild swing at Eberhard Bethge for having spoken of Bonhoeffer's "naive Biblicism." In Huntemann's eyes—and this vision countered that of the mainstream of Bonhoeffer advocates as well as that of his most conservative critics—he had "broken the mental dead end of modern schools of theological thought with his dialectical-dynamic and multidimensional outlook." Above all, in such eyes, including Huntemann's, he was to be seen as "a challenger of modernism."[32]

As noted, the category Huntemann borrowed or invented for this moment in the biography of the book is "Christ-mysticism." With it at his disposal, he was able not only to rescue Bonhoeffer for those in Evangelical circles who had been frightened away by the radicals, but to show how the choice to make creative misuse of him could be valuable for fellow Evangelicals. He claimed that the religionless Christ-mystic Bonhoeffer "is very close in spirit to the Evangelicals," for whom Huntemann wrote. "He will be their church father in the future—or else the evangelicals have no future. Bonhoeffer is in fact so similar to the evangelicals that it will become uncomfortable for them." His theology, thought Huntemann, could bring "the necessary catharsis for the 'evangelicals of all lands,'" a catharsis that, while cleansing, would also hurt.[33]

Given Huntemann's obsession with feminism as the root of many other "evils" of contemporary times, one may well ask, "Why devote so much attention to him? Some other evangelicals and conservatives did not have that crusade on their agenda. Still others among them worked their way past the poles of conservatism and modernism without going through contortions like inventing the choice of "Christ-mysticism," which Huntemann borrowed from Albert Schweitzer. It was a category not picked up by other Evangelicals or other Bonhoeffer students, but it is illustrative of efforts to make Bonhoeffer "work" among some Evangelicals. Here is Huntemann:

> [Christ-mysticism] is in no way comparable to some kind of secular or even Hindu mystical God-experience. Christ-mysticism means that the Christian takes part in the life and death and resurrection of Christ. And so he gains this access to the reality of Christ through encounter with Christ in the word of proclamation. Christ-mysticism does not, therefore, mean to discover a Christ in the depth of one's soul. It means participating in the reality of the Christ who encounters me and takes me in tow, incorporating me into his reality. Albert Schweitzer also expresses the view that Luther was a Christ mystic in the sense that the doctrine of justification was only secondary alongside his understanding of dying and rising with Christ.[34]

For all his idiosyncratic emphases, however, Huntemann illustrates how important it was for some conservatives to wrestle with central issues posed by Bonhoeffer and critically to appropriate him. Perhaps most of all, he stated the case for continuity in the theological program of Bonhoeffer, which is an important case. He simply opposed all those who stressed that in the late letters the author experienced a rupture with his whole theological past and either ignored or repudiated it.

As for those who thought that there was a breach between the early and later Bonhoeffer, Huntemann was typically emphatic in countering them: the interpretation that found such a breach was "completely wrong." What philosopher Martin Heidegger once said, he thought, proved to be true also of Bonhoeffer. "Every person has but one dominant thought. In Bonhoeffer there is change, development, growth, drama, struggle—but never a fundamental break with what went before." He cited letters from Bonhoeffer that helped support his case, however mutedly. Bonhoeffer on August 23, 1944, wrote that he professed to be "traveling with gratitude and cheerfulness along the road where I'm being led,"[35] and that satisfied this Evangelical.

Ask Huntemann what he thought Bonhoeffer contended for most in church and culture and his answer would be clear: order. It may be painting with too broad a brush to elevate the concern for order to front rank among the concerns of Evangelicals in Europe or America, but as they looked out at chaos and sometimes wild innovation, they did promote order. Bonhoeffer gave Huntemann and others among them plenty of references. While critics on the left saw Bonhoeffer as a man of privilege, ethically blinded by his family experience and means, Huntemann saw him as a product and cherisher of order over against chaos and factionalism. The case of Georg Huntemann illustrates how the varieties of scholars discovered in these unfinished letter-sequences something of what they were looking for, as they in their response to the book add color to our biography of it.

Catholicism and modern Evangelicalism in Europe and North America would have represented alien soil to neo-orthodox theologians back in 1945, when the condemned Dietrich Bonhoeffer wrote his last letters and papers from prison. As they changed and as the book *Letters and Papers from Prison* traveled their way for half a century and more, sometimes enthusiastically and sometimes warily, significant leaders among them showed that they and the book were strangers no more.

Travels around the World

CHAPTER 7

The biography of the book *Letters and Papers from Prison* quite naturally accents its travels. Librarians and booksellers catalog and remember it as one of the most traveled books in the field of religion. To discipline our tracking of the book's biography, we have had to stay close to the prosaic ground, finding it difficult to do justice to the ways it took off and fed imaginations of fiction writers, film producers, and others who do not have to stay close to the trail that is often called "literal" or to tell stories once described as "objective." This biography would fall short of its intentions if it failed to remind readers of the reach of the prison letters. It is noteworthy that most of the esthetic and dramatic treatments deal less with the whole life of Bonhoeffer than with the theologian's final two years, the time of his confinement. He did not stop being a theologian, though he helped change concepts of what being one meant. Yet playwrights and filmmakers in their imagination visit him more in his little places of confinement, under the marks of punishment and death.

Rather than attempt a canvass, which could not do justice to the catalog, I will simply sketch some expressions of which I became almost casually aware, meaning that I was not part of one of the popular Bonhoeffer Tours, visits to sites associated with the theologian. As long ago as 1961 I saw Elizabeth Berryhill's *The Cup of Trembling*, a play that—one says "of course"—includes prison scenes. Friend Al Skaggs has tirelessly taken a monological version of it on the road and acted on numberless stages, in scenes that find the prison settings most revelatory. Martin Doblmeier has made an award-winning documentary again stressing the final seasons of the prisoner's life. It is hard to get close to the Bonhoeffer story without being called to read the prison novels, which I do not admire, and the prison poetry, which I do. My fellow graduate student decades ago, Ted Kleinhans, involved me in many discussions as he wove the plot of a novel around the latter days of the prisoner. My "Bonhoeffer shelf" has examples of fiction about the rare theologian whose life-drama attracted novelists. Stephen R. Haynes, whose *The Bonhoeffer Phenomenon* is an ambitious and rewarding reference to "portraits of a Protestant saint," comments on films, plays, and novels and points to pilgrimages and tours that dedicated Bonhoeffer readers may undertake. But aware that we must keep feet on the ground and deal with the life of the book, we hit the road with the book, beginning at its home, in Germany.

Home for Dietrich Bonhoeffer was, successively, the German Empire, the Weimar Republic, the Third Reich—and, posthumously, an unmarked place where his ashes were dumped into a stream in what became the German Democratic Republic, "East Germany." The author of *Letters and Papers from Prison* as a prisoner could not travel. He was confined to prison-yard exercise and then, at the end, he walked the few yards to the gallows, months after he had sent out the last letter. His books, however, can and do make journeys to wherever books are marketed or loaned and read.

Bonhoeffer's book did and does make its way far from theological libraries, far from the German-speaking world, far from the classrooms where it could and sometimes did become assigned reading. Those who trace the Bonhoeffer influence have no difficulty finding records from which they could fill scrapbooks and filing drawers. Necessarily limiting the space devoted to this book's travels, I will point to a few stops along the way, stops chosen in the light of what they can do to illustrate the scope and appeal of the book. We shall see that at many places people read out of or into the letters responses to questions that may not have been accented by Bonhoeffer, but which illustrate his influence. As with lives, so with books: writing their biographies brings one into contact with many who are reached serendipitously, accidentally, and sometimes frontally.

Most books simply stay at home, because they lack cosmopolitan appeal or are intended only for specialists. The author of a directory to a small city in North Dakota does not expect such a book to be a best-seller, make a mark, or even be noticed in South Carolina, South Korea, or even South Dakota. Committees who might be called to prepare a booklet for the membership list of First Presbyterian Church in an Indiana city in 1945 would never expect to make sales in Slovenia. It is possible that someone doing genealogical work may track down such provincial or specialized books, but they are not likely to create a market, and no one expects such a book to change lives.

Some writings that are obscure at birth do have a delayed effect. For example, *The Diary of Anne Frank* or works by survivors of the Holocaust and others that elicit humanistic interest in prison literature about that horror have inspired any number of diaries, letters, or drafts of books composed behind barbed wire and under the noses of vigilant guards who looked on from towers along the walls. Similarly, the rather small number of African American slaves who somehow learned to read and write left behind some narratives of their conversions, stories that they cannot have pictured would win a diverse readership but were much later collected in anthologies and are staples in curricula across the nation or used by activist groups promoting racial justice.

Reasons for the eventual and then sudden appeal of *Letters and Papers from Prison* were obvious.

Proverbially a prophet who was relatively without honor in his own country, Bonhoeffer meanwhile was being honored, and the book Bethge edited and promoted was being received on several continents. It found a readership among hundreds of thousands of people who probably had never before bought a book by a contemporary theologian, a book whose index, as we have noted, included names that were obscure or off-putting. As the life of the book exerted new influence, scholars assessed the reasons for the appeal. Among serious theologians—the people who set the terms at and after midcentury, many of whose names started with a "B"—Barth, Berdyaev, Brunner, Buber, Bultmann, and all the rest—Bonhoeffer was, or at least seemed to be, the most accessible. Some had known his prewar writings and now were fascinated with and engrossed in the adventure of following the turns his prison letters revealed, another fact that added to their allure.

A second reason for the international appeal was the fact that it included poems, prayers, and short treatises—one for a marriage, one for a baptism—which translated well, given the artistry and personal story of the author. Christians who were starved for stories of heroism if not sainthood would have cherished the book on those devotional, liturgical, and theological terms alone. They provided and still supply a large readership after two-thirds of a century, even though Hitler, the Nazis, and the Resistance survive in the living memory of ever fewer people.

New issues—the Cold War, terrorism, and the like—have crowded the memories and taken their place on the agendas four and five generations after the Tegel prison story was current.

The third reason for the book to travel and be reckoned with had to do with its message of liberation. In the century of revolutionary turmoil it was picked up for its message of freedom in struggles in South Africa, the United States, and wherever literate Christians participated in struggles for freedom and justice.

Finally, however, it was the latter-day radical probes and visions that began with Bonhoeffer's letters to Bethge that inspired controversy and still fires it. "Who is Jesus Christ for us today?" is as enlivening a question in Cape Town as it is in Korea. Has the world truly "come of age" because, on Bonhoeffer's terms of description, it appears to have done so in most of his Western Europe? Or does the experience of religious growth, vitality, and even explosion in much of the world call his story of the "adulthood" of the world and secularization into question? What sense does it make to say that Christianity was to turn out to be and by now ought to be "religionless," divorced from metaphysics, piety, and ecstasy? All this at a time when Christian growth is most visible precisely where it was expected to have been blunted? Instead of observing only smooth transitions to modernity and away from fanaticism, how can analysts account for religious enthusiasms, on one hand, and hard-line fundamentalisms on the other, as these gained followings among the literalist-minded?

Just as stories of travels and adventures log the travails and triumph of celebrated authors, they usually depict the dramas of people who welcomed them far from the places and contexts of their origins. Books and their authors, however, on occasion have more difficulty making their way "back home" than they do winning support from far away. When locals read reminiscences of another's childhood in "their" town, they may respond with a variety of reactions. Often these will include notes of pride. Just as often one will hear phrases such as "Who does she think she is?" or "That's not at all the way it was; this is distorted."

Hanfried Müller and Georg Huntemann, on the left and on the right, in the GDR and DDR, East and West, do not represent the full variety of major responses in the Germanys that represent the "back home" of *Letters and Papers from Prison*. In the DDR, West Germany, the book was not always and everywhere the object of pride among citizens on many levels and of many stripes. Some were critical scholars and church leaders, many of them rivals in the reputation game that Bonhoeffer did not survive to get to play. These commentators tracked references they could use to diminish the increasingly heroic-appearing Bonhoeffer and his lauded book. Germans who kept their eye on these things knew that this resister of the Nazis as a young theologian had not gained credentials by having been present at the Barmen Synod of

1934, in which the Confessing Church made its bold claims for the faith and against the regime. His absence counted against him among some confessors or those who identified with Barmen when the war was over. In the prison letters, Bonhoeffer provided targets to other clerics who would attack him after he spoke with disappointment about the conservative turn the church had taken in recent years. Academically, he had held no tenured chair at any university. As for his earlier books, the professorial critics considered most of his postdoctoral writings to have been drawn from sermons and not lectures, issued in relatively small occasional books, and thus not candidates for serious dissection.

Bonhoeffer's career, evidences of which show up repeatedly in *Letters and Papers from Prison*, suggested that there had been more restlessness than continuity in his life. He had traveled to Spain and England and America, with a foray into Mexico for a conference. Such trips provided little opportunity for him to nurture friendships, and he was somewhat reserved among most of those he met, though they were drawn to him. In the few short years of his university and postgraduate study he was seldom tied to a place more than one season at a time. Who could take him seriously, some asked, as a professorial author, since he held classes, intense but informal as they were, only at a remote distance in the farm country? Not much could be said in the letters about his ecumenical contacts, since they were so often linked with conspiratorial and resistance work, about which the less said, the better, and nothing said, the best of all. These ties did take him to England, Sweden, and Switzerland, but in each case too briefly to count for much in conventional church unity circles. Conference-going critics noted, with some warrant, that, while Bonhoeffer was good at building relations, he was on the scene nowhere long enough to become a part of sustained dialogue. We also have to notice that many of his travels and other experiences occurred before *Letters and Papers from Prison* appeared, so they belong to the biography of the author, not of the book.

Returning to the immediate context of the book, one can eavesdrop on conversations about it on the author's home front. Some of those who measured theological reputations had become irritated when they heard his name mentioned along with those of the giants Karl Barth and Rudolf Bultmann, as if he ranked with them. True, it became known that he had been in correspondence with Barth, but he was clearly the junior partner, not the prime agent who stirred interest and built up expectations among those who mattered. After the war, when it was learned that he had been implicated in the attempt to assassinate Hitler, many German clergy, even as their generation abhorred anything Hitlerian, still were not in the habit of honoring would-be assassins. Many of Bonhoeffer's contemporaries did not want to be reminded of the enormities and horrors of the Nazi period, or to work through their own positions of half-guilt and half-innocence with him as a mirror. At the end of such a canvass one has to conclude that if anything of Bonhoeffer's final and decisive years was to survive and be spread, it would depend on one person, old friend Eberhard Bethge, and one genre of writing, "letters and papers."

Some good fortune did come editor Bethge's way after 1950 when Germans who, also to satisfy interests of the Allied nations, started settling accounts by bringing some Nazi criminals to justice. In one startling exchange in court, an SS man on trial, Colonel Walter Huppenkothen, had to take the stand as he tried to defend himself against the accusation that he had, without warrant or any sense of justice, been the one who sentenced and sent Bonhoeffer to the gallows. The trial was as messy as so many were in the chaotic time when Germans who were accused of war crimes were vying with each other in efforts to exonerate themselves. The upside of the disgrace was that it gave Bethge many opportunities to learn and correct the historical record and gather new materials for his biographical work. Huppenkothen was tried three times but was let off because he pleaded, successfully in the eyes of the court, that he had simply been following law. Law, of course, said that anyone who tried to kill the head of state had to risk and probably should receive the death penalty. Such stigma in the eyes of many Germans, born as it was of ambiguity about law and ethics, justice and revolution, lasted long. In fact it was almost forty years—from 1956 to 1995—before a German court finally saw clear to declare posthumously that Bonhoeffer had been innocent.[1]

A further complication that made acceptance of the book difficult in some West German circles was the fact that in the bitter Cold War years, theologians like Hanfried Müller and the Weisensee circle found it easy to employ its plot for ideological purposes. Some who resented Bonhoeffer and his book used that appropriation and the distortions to suggest that the book had to be seriously flawed, if it was so vulnerable to such interpretations. Others refused to take seriously a theological treatise in the form of letters; they were used to more formal, multivolume treatises shaped over a whole career. There were bigger problems, however, based in issues that were not easily resolved and in conflicts that were too deeply rooted to be lightly overcome.

Some of the objections in the home base were political and cultural. Technically, we remind ourselves, the author *had* been a traitor. Word trickled out and then was expanded in wide journalistic coverage that author Bonhoeffer had indeed been, at least on some levels, a participant in the conspiracy to kill Hitler. Despised though Hitler was among so many Germans during the decades of their recovery post-Nazism, they had no principled base for forgiving or "pardoning" a theologian and his circle for what an earlier age would have called tyrannicide. To his executioners he had been simply recorded as "an Enemy of the State."

Add to that still another complication: Bonhoeffer was a Lutheran, as was the West German Protestant majority. For much of four centuries Lutherans had been taught, and most believed, that Christians were not to resist government in any of its forms. If there was one biblical text on this theme that was drummed into the minds of confirmands and preached by pastors, it was the word in the thirteenth chapter of Paul's Letter to the Romans declaring that "the powers that be"—Nero back then, Hitler in the recent past—were ordained of God. Whoever resisted them would receive judgment.

Events in the first postwar years illustrate the uneasiness over or disdain toward the author of *Letters and Papers from Prison*. His own church in Berlin-Brandenburg did have the grace to honor the also-executed Pastor Paul Schneider, who matched Bonhoeffer for courage as he simply witnessed for the faith in his preaching. But he had not been in on the conspiracy against the head of state. Words such as "this church could never approve of the plot of July 20, whatever its purpose may have been" would have been a sufficient indictment, but the church leaders added, perhaps gratuitously, "that amongst those who have suffered in consequence were countless persons who never wished this attempted assassination to take place."[2]

Bonhoeffer's father received a letter from the clergy in Bielefeld, explaining: "A number of names have been chosen of men who became victims of National

Socialism, among them Paul Schneider (Dickenschied) and your son Dietrich. We the pastors of this town, have grave misgivings about the choice of both these names, as we should not like the names of our fellow pastors who died for their faith to appear side by side with political martyrs." They wanted to draw a strict line between "church" as they defined it and "state," also in their definition, and Bonhoeffer and Schneider were therefore people of "state," whom the church could neglect or despise.[3]

While a church across the channel in postwar England came to be named after Bonhoeffer, a large German regional church even went out of its way to forbid its parishes to name a new church after him. The existence of *Letters and Papers from Prison* was evidently not moving or convincing enough to warrant the presence of a bishop of standing to be on the scene when a tablet honoring Bonhoeffer was dedicated at Flossenburg, where he had been killed. The problem for them was also that in their eyes the plaque carried the name of a "political, not a Christian martyr."

That there had been other resisters with whom Bonhoeffer was acquainted was evident between the lines of his letters. He dared not name names in his communications. After the war the stories of his subversive contacts in the years before and during hostilities became more familiar. Some of them were well-known. On June 30, 1944, in a single closing line of a letter to Bethge, Bonhoeffer remembered having been with his friend at "Martin's." This Martin Niemoeller, an early resister, who was better known than Bonhoeffer at the time of his writing, a date that, Bonhoeffer noted, was the seventh year to the day after Niemoeller's arrest.[4] While the Tegel prisoner eventually became a virtual celebrity as a symbol of resistance and dissent in the name of church and Christ, he was also long treated as suspect for having worked against the government.

Beyond those two obvious factors were others with which Bethge had to deal. These letters reflected a church situation in a secular world, and they used theological language in a Germany where the public was drifting from church and theology. And there was also the matter of the format of the manuscript. Called to the mission of spreading the fame of Bonhoeffer and circulating his letters, Bethge and his wife Renate considered it a hard sell to interest people at home or far away in letters and scraps of writings that issued from the confining cell. Paradoxically, however, it was the very prison context that came to inspire curiosity about and fascination with the book, to the point that some said it contributed to a "Bonhoeffer myth."

A tiny but eye-catching footnote in de Gruchy's book notes that, remarkably, Jewish journals eventually published some reviews of the Bonhoeffer book.[5] One of these notices appeared in the popular press *Allgemeine Wochenzeitung der Juden in Deutschland*, and another appeared in a publication in Zürich. While the second of these was published virtually across the river and beyond the border from Germany, its appearance suggests that curiosity about the author of the letters was drawing some international and interreligious attention. However, most of the debate about Bonhoeffer vis-à-vis Judaism dealt with his writings from the 1930s, since, as we noted, the prison letters were not a forum or format in which Bonhoeffer could develop and express views of contemporary Jews.

Beyond Europe, African and Other Movements of Liberation

A sketchy and quick world tour, which is intended to be and can be no more than a sampler—the literature is vast—could properly begin in South Africa, so far from Tegel prison and yet a land full of prisons in which opponents of a murderous and racist regime had been long locked up. One reason for beginning with this choice of a remote (from Europe) site is the fact that the International Dietrich Bonhoeffer Society held one of its quadrennial congresses there to attract scholars who do comparative work. A second is the presence of Professor de Gruchy, who, it should be clear to readers by now, has been through the decades involved with international Bonhoeffer studies. He was himself a participant in the church-based struggles against apartheid and for freedom, and both as an activist and a scholar he and his colleagues modeled many of their acts and interpretations on insights gained from reading *Letters and Papers from Prison*.

In 1979, when apartheid policies still dominated, de Gruchy wrote *The Church Struggle in South Africa* and then seconded it with *Bonhoeffer and South Africa: Theology in Dialogue* in 1984. In the South Africa of 1979 there had not been many reasons for those seeking liberation to put much energy into hoping for better times. Among the leaders, however, de Gruchy chose to cite the Bonhoeffer letters to inspire hope. He reminded his readers that Bonhoeffer, in an even more deadly situation than theirs, criticized cynics who, he wrote, "think that the meaning of present events is chaos, disorder and catastrophe." They thought so in part, he wrote, because they had no concern for the future but were instead "consumed by the present moment." In the book published in 1984 he reported that so directly did Bonhoeffer's life and letters apply to the apparently different South African scene that one innocent asked Bethge in a seminar there, "When did Bonhoeffer visit South Africa? He knows our situation from the inside!"[6]

South African activists and theologians have often made the point that they could not simply import, adapt, and impose theology and strategy from Europe and North America. The African expressions have an autochthonous character; that is, they have grown up out of the soil and soul of Africa. Yet *Letters and Papers from Prison* showed readers there that the two very diverse theological contexts shared a biblical basis with the experiences of the oppressed wherever Christians have suffered. At the same time, de Gruchy insisted, readers must learn the particular history, the record of their past church life—Anglican and "Dutch" Reformed—in order to break free and overcome oppressors in their own time. When in the course of time they did reach further for resources, *Letters and Papers from Prison* was in demand.

The Bonhoeffer scholars, not sentimentalists, are a critical group, much given to "the hermeneutics of suspicion." This means that most of them in their academic writings began inquiries by calling into question applications of *Letters and Papers from Prison* and whatever else in the Bonhoeffer legacy might apply to themselves. They followed by engaging in questioning. In 1996 the Bonhoeffer Congress, meeting in Cape Town, asked the question the prisoner had posed about himself, his colleagues, his generation, and their situation: "Are We Still of Any Use?" To no one's surprise, the introducer of the question was veteran de Gruchy, who asked whether it could be said that Bonhoeffer "is still of significance for us today as we stand on the brink of a new millennium in a rapidly changing world." While Bonhoeffer had anticipated change, de Gruchy noted, "even he could not have foreseen the extent of those changes in places like South Africa, and the crises and challenges which would accompany them." De Gruchy had to ponder what serious students of Bonhoeffer's letters and papers had to ask and what critics always do as they trace the ups and downs in the life of this book: is this interest in him "anything more than nostalgic loyalty to a remarkable person" and, I add, anything more than devotion to his remarkable book?[7]

De Gruchy observed that many of the ambiguous and morally complicated acts in South African liberation and its aftermath led him to ask, "Should we, many of us compromised by past events, now stand aside and let others take on the task of building a new nation?" Bonhoeffer, he thought, "would have had to ask his question as the Confessing Church and the church in East Germany took its own ambiguous course." Had not the time for Christianity in the Western world as a whole run its course? If there was to be renewal, would it not come from "beyond Christendom," from India, Latin America, and Africa? De Gruchy, seeking to be honest and realistic, asked, "Is it possible that the church in South Africa can overcome that tainted past and truly make a contribution to the shaping of the new South Africa?"[8]

In a separate essay, he brought up another point that was becoming controversial in the life of Bonhoeffer's book. He noted that the legacy so far had been largely in the hands of leaders who, from the viewpoint of the churches beyond Christendom, had left them with the question, not of the usefulness of his theology, "but about the future role of those elites of which he was a part." After de Gruchy heard the mix of voices among congress participants, he did not have answers. Instead he said what people in the trail of the life of the book characteristically have said— that it and the congress had "enabled the dialogue with Bonhoeffer to continue," in that case in South Africa, but elsewhere as well.[9]

De Gruchy, as editor of the book from and about the congress, gave the final word to H. Russel Botman, who had been rapporteur at the Cape Town conference. Botman was not the first African to connect Bonhoeffer with South Africa. Among "Colored" theologians, for instance, Alan Boesak, for a time among the most influential ecumenical and activist leaders in the nation, made explicit reference to Bonhoeffer's influence. In 1988, at the Fifth International Bonhoeffer Congress, he spoke on "What Dietrich Bonhoeffer Has Meant to Me." Boesak could compare his experiences with Bonhoeffer's, for he had also been imprisoned for his resistance to oppression. Like Bonhoeffer in his prison days, he craved helpful reading material, including, in his case, Bethge's biography of Bonhoeffer. In his recall of the prison time, and remembering Bonhoeffer's earlier influence on him back in the academy, he said he had let Bonhoeffer speak to him, "no longer in the academic background in Kampen, but in the silence of my cell for the one day that I was allowed to read." Boesak urged his listeners from around the world, gathered at Cape Town, to read Bonhoeffer, who so effectively combined theology with "the meaning of struggle, the meaning of identification with those who are voiceless, the meaning of participating in the battles of this world that seek to establish justice and peace and humanity."[10]

Now Botman, representing the newer generation of blacks, was given the task of asking one last time for that conference and about the book, "Is Bonhoeffer Still of Any Use in South Africa?" He spoke from experience he gained at the University of Western Cape, where only 1.2 percent of the 14,560 students at the time were white. The ethos on that campus was not nonreligious but interreligious, with Muslims and diverse kinds of Christians making up the largest groups in residence. As four members of that community spoke at the end of the Congress, Botman condensed the question or topic each of the four posed: "*Who* are we?" "*Where* are we situating the question? "*When* is the time for the question?" and "*To whom* are we called to be of use?" Such questions could as well be asked in Berlin, Harlem, Seoul, or New Delhi, about a book and its author who had spoken so clearly to Germany before World War II.[11]

Botman, in his report of the congress, included a summary of his own talk, which took off from Bonhoeffer's little essay titled "After Ten Years." It had appeared at the beginning of *Letters and Papers from Prison*. "We will have to face the challenge raised" there, Botman said, and then asked: "Will our inward power of resistance be strong enough, and our honesty with ourselves remorseless enough, for us to find our way back to simplicity and straightforwardness?" In Botman's mind, the fact that Bonhoeffer's book was still capable of raising the right questions was evidenced across the generational lines. Bonhoeffer had written, "Thinking and acting for the sake of the coming generation, but being ready to go any day without fear or anxiety—that, in practice, is the spirit in which we are forced to live."[12]

Liberation in South America

The voice of Botman in South Africa, in his appreciation and critique alike, represents attitudes toward Bonhoeffer among those identified with Liberation Theology as a movement on several continents. Most historians of the movement treat Bonhoeffer as a sort of founder, or at least as a theologian whose late prison writings had traveled to liberationists and been used by them. At the same time, they took their most noted form in the decades after his death, and they accepted agendas he could not have anticipated. In such cases, the features of Bonhoeffer's letters, papers, and life left him—for all the sacrifices made, including with his life—as imprisoned in bourgeois Western culture. So he rarely received a free ride in Africa, Latin America, and Asia among liberationists. They wanted to reinterpret biblical and theological motifs to show what was called "God's preferential option for the poor"—which, though coined after his death, certainly would not have been a problem phrase for Bonhoeffer—and to make use of radical, often Marxist, social thought and leverage.

While Bonhoeffer was becoming an appreciated figure in Latin America, theologians on the scene have always been quick to point out that many elements in the prison letters were not easily translatable to later liberation fronts, and sometimes the limits they perceived in Bonhoeffer were even inhibiting. Such a charge demands a hearing and bears examining. Thus Ivan Petrella, in *Beyond Liberation Theology: A Polemic*, published after the prime of the liberation movement in 2008, needed only two pages to summarize the case involving Bonhoeffer. For him and those with whom he identified or whom he represented, the chosen theme for criticism was "idolatry." The word had not gained mention as an index reference in *Letters and Papers from Prison*, but it now came to be seen as the main issue. Petrella, a seasoned writer on Liberation Theology, quoted with favor Gustavo Gutiérrez, who, in the eyes of many, was the prime liberationist. Gutiérrez had written that Bonhoeffer's concept of "a religionless world" placed him "at the cusp of liberation theology."

Then Petrella seconded the motion with a decisive quotation from *Letters and Papers from Prison* on a point important on the South American Catholic scene, where the church often was seen as "otherworldly." He saw Bonhoeffer on this point as a corrective, since he showed that the Christian hope of resurrection, which brings a person "back to his life on earth," is not a "mythological hope." For causes of liberation, Petrella quoted Bonhoeffer: "It is not the religious act that makes the Christian, but participation in the sufferings of God in the secular life. . . . Jesus calls men, not to a new religion, but to life."[13] So liberation theologians responded, Petrella stressed, when they read that Bonhoeffer believed that Jesus's call to life has an "irreducible physical component." As before, we can say "so far so good, but not far enough," whatever the first impressions might be.

At times Petrella continued to express satisfaction, because Bonhoeffer, he wrote, "even comes close to the liberationist premise that theology must be done from the perspective of the poor and the oppressed." He cited the author of the prison letters one more time in a text that countered what some of the South African liberationists had contended on the matter of elites: "We have for once learnt to see the great events of world history from below, from the perspective of the outcast, the suspects, the maltreated, the powerless, the oppressed, the reviled—in short, from the perspective of those who suffer." One might consider that conclusion the basis of liberationist perspectives.[14]

Before he let himself get carried away, Petrella showed that he favored a more radical perspective, this from Franz Hinkelammert, who argued that Bonhoeffer let "the world" off too easily when he set out to denounce idolatry in the church. It was deficient and thus wrong, said this critic, when Bonhoeffer almost passingly questioned whether idolatry was any longer an important category in a religionless world. Idols, he had written, "are worshipped, and idolatry implies that people still worship something. But we don't worship anything now, not even idols." Not so, countered Hinkelammert, for the evidence of idolatry, he argued, was a central charge in Liberation Theology, where theologians in church of old and world of new, Hinkelammert observed, suggested that a world that has emancipated itself from God "produces its own religion and its own idols. Bonhoeffer's belief that this world lacks religion and believes in nothing is striking.... He himself lies before an enormous idol that [*sic*] under which he will be sacrificed. But he doesn't see it as such, because he understands idolatry as falling exclusively within the ecclesial sphere, and not in the wider world."

In the course of this argument Petrella and those who shared the liberationist view of secular power provided one of the most telling critiques of Bonhoeffer, or at least of those who had what I would call romantic or utopian views of the world that considers itself to be secular, adult, coming of age. The summary judgment: "Today ... the most dangerous religions and theologies, those that affect the life chances of the greatest number of people, are not found in churches or the traditionally religious sphere, but outside of it, in what is usually mistakenly understood as the secular world." Such judgments can be viewed as among the most searching in the critique of the worldview Bonhoeffer had seen was emerging. We might consider the insight to be a prophetic gift from "poor world" theologians to those who, more than they knew, had been produced within or had bought into the ethos and outlook of the prosperous West—and, if Petrella is right—a West that is prone to idolatry.[15]

Even Asian Contexts

Whoever continues a tour of places outside Europe and North America, observing how in the life of the book Bonhoeffer criticism followed, might turn next to Asia. East Asian Protestants in many cases are conservative supporters of economic systems that Latin American liberationists like Hinkelammert considered to be the producers of enticing idolatries. The Asian nation with the largest percentage of Christians, South Korea, for example, includes a church population that is in many cases supportive of untrammeled economic enterprise. The largest Christian congregation in the world, one that combines messages of personal physical prosperity with affirmations of nationalism, is in Korea. Little in its message confirms the observation that in the eyes of its leaders and adherents, the world had come of age, that Christianity was to be presented in a religionless construct, or that the church should survive and be reborn as existing "for others." While such churches as this giant may be exceptions in prospering Korean Christian circles, their presence and prosperity would disconfirm impressions many took from Bonhoeffer's letters.

It would, however, be misleading to describe the Korean church (or Japanese, Philippine, Indonesian, or Indian church, for samples) as being of one mind and outlook. If in Latin American liberation movements some thought that Bonhoeffer did not do justice to the need for struggles against idolatry in economic and civil spheres, a voice from the Asian context charged, not without reason, that his writings were not immediately useful in the cause of the liberation of women. Again in this instance Bonhoeffer was both used as an inspirer and scored for his sometimes gross limitations on the feminism front. To illustrate this case, we will listen not to a mild and concessive figure but to a determinedly jarring radical liberationist.

Turning to Chung Hyun Kyung, then a professor at Ewha Women's University in Korea and later a professor at New York's Union Theological Seminary, does not mean that we have discerned what is most typical, but it is among the most radical. Referencing her Cape Town speech and essay also is a way of showing that not all is light and sweetness when students of Bonhoeffer come together.

Right off, Professor Chung blasted Bonhoeffer's concept of Jesus as the "man for others." Was there room, she asked pointedly, for "woman for others"? Or for *Asian* women for others? For that matter, she even had trouble with the very concept of others." Many in her feminist company, she claimed, considered talk of "the other" to be part of the ideological core of patriarchy. To her in Asia "the other" came across as a conceptual flaw: "There is no 'other.' I am you, and you are me."[16]

Bonhoeffer's stress on "following Jesus" meant "suffering and martyrdom" for him and his followers, but the ideology of suffering in Christian culture, she argued, had been and was being used to domesticate people who possessed lesser power. Korean women of her outlook, she wrote, did not want to "glorify the suffering death of a messiah," but to abolish all kinds of capital punishment. Remembering the question he had asked in the prison letters, "are we still of any use?" she answered, "Maybe we Christians will be of some use, but only if we deconstruct our Christendom, Christian superiority, Christian cultural imperialism, and christocentric mentalities."

America, and Racial Movements
in the United States

Letters and Papers from Prison, in its many bindings, editions, and translations, traveled so far, so often, so swiftly, to so many places, leaving so many different effects on diverse readers and readerships, that it is impossible to do justice to its full career. An effort to be comprehensive would result in a kind of unalphabetized gazetteer and would add little to the understanding of the book's scope and influence beyond what words like "myriad," "plethora," "many," and "multi-" point to. Therefore we have to select, to view the terrain it covers as if from a great distance, so only the boldest and, one hopes, somehow representative and revealing features stand out. In the present case, one could canvass the literature and look for how the book has been treated in the United States by Hispanic or Native American people—though in those two cases the researcher would come up with the answer: not very much.

Others cannot be bypassed, however, and the examples from Africa, Latin America, and Asia can demonstrate how diverse the issues are. On those terms, "Liberation" in the context of African Americans surely should have an important place. It happens that the civil rights movement and the three-and-a-half-century-late moves toward assuring equality for blacks occurred in the decades when Bonhoeffer's book was informing a variety of endeavors to secure rights. Bonhoeffer from prison, like African American leaders, spoke constantly of freedom. One sees this theme in numerous book titles about Bonhoeffer. The witness came, somehow, out of a particular Protestant tradition. Readers of Bonhoeffer and followers of Martin Luther King, Jr., were summoned to biblically based reflection on how freedom is attained. Both had to deal with a world long perceived as religious—one thinks of the many civil rights leaders who had a "Reverend" attached to their name.

The blacks who did make much of Bonhoeffer found bridges still to cross. To pick one of the most extensive and thoughtful among bridge-building books, I would turn to *No Difference in the Fare: Dietrich Bonhoeffer and the Problem of Racism*,[17] authored by Josiah Ulysses Young III, a professor at Wesley Theological

Seminary in Washington, D.C. Young would have lost all credentials in African American theological circles and would have shown that he was blind to cultural tensions and deaf to conflicting voices on the racial justice front had he not begun by showing how hard it was to deal with some texts in the letters and papers. He pointed to them at the very beginning when he observed that a Bonhoeffer wedding sermon in the book was "a bit sexist." Chung Hyun Kyung would have said, simply, "sexist." Other texts in his letters reveal that Bonhoeffer was in some ways what one of his critics on the far left called an elitist and an "anti-democrat"—that's a bit strong—who had trouble dealing with chaos in his time and "the loss of belief in the divine right of social structures."[18] Was he paternalist? Yes. "Indeed, Bonhoeffer's view as to why the New Testament is soft on slavery," found in the *Ethics* which he was writing concurrently with the prison letters, "might well make an African-American think Bonhoeffer had made common cause with the master." He "never disowned his bourgeois ballasts—his moorings in Berlin's upper crust." The theologian, Young pointed out critically, had even enjoyed some middle-class amenities in his early days in prison.[19] All those charges were familiar by the time Young wrote, but when the book traveled to Harlem or to Howard University, it inspired fresh reviews and comments from a perspective not likely to have been used in Germany. Many of his historical judgments were reflective of a life lived in a different time and became problematic in another time and place. In sum, in Bonhoeffer's writings, even from prison, there *were* expressions of "chauvinism," "privilege," and "Eurocentric perspective," and these all counted against him among liberationists.[20] Bonhoeffer, we are led to judge, had been born in the wrong place and the wrong time and the wrong context for him to be as wise as those, coming along later, who were born in the right place and the right time in the right contexts to judge him.[21]

Credit Young for laying the charges on the table and then picking up the cards and playing them in a thoughtful essay. He and his subject did come from two different worlds and two different half-centuries. To make his point, Young testified about an encounter with two pastors in a Pentecostal church, the Sanctified Church in New York. Even the names of the constellation of Pentecostal churches of which they were a part suggest more than terminological incompatibilities; "their church was one of the holyroller churches that made up the Soul Saving Station." One might have thought—indeed, Young himself at first thought— that these pastors would have been far removed from Bonhoeffer, "the world-class, highly privileged, highly accomplished German theologian." They were African Americans "overwhelmed by racial injustice; and in desperation they reached for his theological insight, ... even though much about him appears to have been chauvinistic." Surprise! Young was amazed as he reported that the black ministers he encountered had studied Bonhoeffer in seminary "and felt he had lived out the meaning of the gospel—a meaning akin to the reason their congregation danced and shouted in church every Sunday and several days during the rest of the week."[22]

When discussing Bonhoeffer's critique of the concept and practices of religion, Young noted: "Far more important than doctrine is prayer and righteous action" among persons. "*The fare is cheap and all can go.*" The italicized words were part of the title of Young's book, but not the end of that sentence. It went on: "Ponder Africa." Like Ivan Petrella and other liberationists, Young repeated Bonhoeffer's "it is not the religious act that makes the Christian, but participation in the sufferings of God in the secular life."[23] Is that not, he asked, pertinent to the world of the beaten-down African Other?

Young thought that Bonhoeffer was signaling a basic cultural and theological turn.

How in keeping with Bonhoeffer's legacy it would be if wholeness were to entail the turn from the North, meaning the First World, to the South, meaning the Third World (with a focus on Africa). Ernst Feil suggests something similar to this: "Bonhoeffer no longer looked for help in the salvation of Occidental Christianity and Western culture." Such Christianity had already had its day, and, as religions go, was waning. . . . What is more, Bonhoeffer believed that Europe had succumbed to the void.[24]

How accurate were these assessments of the culture out of which the prison letters came? Bonhoeffer's lineage and context are apparent from references in his letters. He was descended from theologians, goldsmiths, doctors, councilors, burgomasters, and his father, professor and psychiatrist and president of the High Court at Tübingen, with his mother a descendant of distinguished theologians. André Dumas had observed that Bonhoeffer's work has undeniably *un accent aristocratique*.[25] Even in prison, his being well-connected is evident in the letters. His cousin had jurisdiction over military prisons, and Bonhoeffer expressed some embarrassment over courtesies and amenities that were his more than they were of other prisoners. Young even agreed with the criticism of Ernst Feil that the world Bonhoeffer had lost and that he saw Europe and "modern man" losing was not the world of these African American pastors, even in their wildest imaginations.[26] His writings gave the impression that "we are *all* so indebted to the Enlightenment," when *we* were not.

Having listed and weighed these honest problems, Young still stepped up: "Yet all these things— Bonhoeffer's chauvinism, privilege, and his Eurocentric perspective—do not in themselves discount his work in my book. Neither would the revelation that he was not quite as taken with blacks as one might think."[27] Young, like so many other nonelite, unprivileged readers felt free to criticize their mentor because his writings gave them license to do so. These encounters on the page between letters or papers and the writings of Bonhoeffer's supporters provide one more chapter in the life of this twentieth-century book, a prompt and a challenge wherever it went. I will let Young, in the final paragraph of his book on cross-cultural encounters and racial realities, quoting a spiritual that provided a title for his book, put his seal on this episode in that life, as it relates to cultures far from Berlin:

> One can only thank Dietrich Bonhoeffer for sealing his witness with unimpeachable integrity. *I* surely thank him for letting his light shine in that way. For his witness—and the witnesses of several others, quick as well as dead—has convinced me that racism is as close to original sin as anything that threatens life today. Our holocausts prove that incontestably. I have the hope that those of us who suffer because this is so will find ways to resist this evil as nobly as Bonhoeffer did. Which is no veiled injunction to plot against racist tyrants. That was *Bonhoeffer's* call. This—*No Difference in the Fare*—is a call to freedom: *Get on board little children.*[28]

Continuity and Change

Biographers look for turning points, basic decisions made, accidents, or other extraordinary events in the lives of their subjects. The biographers of classic books do not have to look for extraordinary events in the lives of such volumes. They present themselves, as if leaping out from the pages or the records of response to each, bidding for attention. Certainly, the story of *Letters and Papers from Prison* features highlights that serve to illuminate the less dramatic aspects of the book. A biographer in the present case has to note the startling origins, the birth of a book in a Nazi prison. That it attracted a following and was interpreted peculiarly on both sides of the East/West political divide during the Cold War has demanded notice. So does its use by sometimes atheist philosophers and theologians. Leaders of liberation movements across the North/South and rich/poor divides wrestled with its meanings and came up with negative as well as positive assessments. The biographer observes and reports on these illuminating encounters and follows the subject into seniority.

As for turning points: most surveyors of the responses to the late writings of Bonhoeffer agree that the contents of his letter to Bethge from Tegel prison dated April 30, 1944, is decisive for appraisers of the career of the book. I will italicize the lead-in to the major theme in that letter, quoting it once more: *"What might surprise or perhaps even worry you would be my theological thoughts and where they are leading . . . . What keeps gnawing at me is the question, what is Christianity, or who is Christ actually for us today?"*[1]

In hundreds, indeed, in many thousands of reviews, arguments, conferences, and initiatives growing out of the book, this letter signals to diverse readers either a turning point to a whole new theological vista or the approach to a dead-ending of a tragic career. Many who celebrate the life and writings of this author of prison letters also cheer the fact that the stir it has created is of a *theological* character. Many books deal with resistance plots against Hitler, prison life under the Nazis and executions by them, or ecumenical engagements in the war years, so this one by Bonhoeffer would not necessarily stand out. It is the dramatic theological emphasis, anticipated in some letters before April 30 and only beginning to be developed immediately thereafter, which preoccupies most discussants.

Bonhoeffer, in one of his papers collected in the book, noted that his generation had no ground to stand on and asked, "Are we still of use?" Since he posed confrontational questions like that one to his friend Bethge and others, he had to begin to answer the question himself, as many of them also chose to do. Central, of course, is his focus on that one insistent question: "Who is Christ actually for us today?" Jews, Muslims, atheists, and those casually attracted to the Bonhoeffer story can view that question from some distance. They do not have to provide an answer to it for themselves, but they live with and might well try to understand their neighbors for whom the question of Christ is urgent. They may read over the shoulder and watch students of Bonhoeffer underlining key passages, while asking questions of their own.

Questions about the Book's Provocations

First among these would be the one that frames the others: *Had* "the world that has come of age" actually *come* of age, as Bonhoeffer judged that it had been doing? Was the author accurate in his description of a new secularity that would replace conventional religiosity, routinized piety, and the world that had apparently not come of age? The corollary to that first observation about the world's maturity was, for Bonhoeffer, a second one. As master theologian Karl Barth before him and now as he himself defined it, religion, ossified but still powerful, was on the defensive, pushed into decline, and destined for obsolescence or for the figurative grave of old cultures. Along with such a farewell to religion and his pondering of its demise came Bonhoeffer's critique of religious institutions and practices, bonded as most of them were to a dying culture. Did this mean that the church and life in community, which had meant so much to him into 1944, were now to be bypassed or rejected?

In many ways, of course, that figurative burial of Christian institutions alone was premature or simply misplaced. Early in the new millennium, decades after he wrote, responsible statisticians estimated that there were 41,000 Christian denominations, almost 4,850,000 congregations or worship centers, and 28,000 major service agencies of the churches. All this added up to a hard-to-miss phenomenon that was displaying signs of life, growth, and innovation. Why speak of Christian institutions as waning leftovers from the world that was supposed to have come of age?[2]

Second, did Bonhoeffer, a consistent person of faith since adolescence and a theologian in his own maturity, who by definition as theologian must necessarily deal in "God-talk," turn his back on all that he had stood for when he pictured believers having to affirm and act "even if there were no God"? Was it "Good-bye, God!" for him, or, if God existed, was God being sent off the world's stage as an irrelevancy? One had to ask: Was there a clear breach between the Bonhoeffer of the years before he wrote as he did in April 1944 and another Bonhoeffer thereafter?

Third, though aware of all the rich options for talking about Jesus Christ that were inherited from twenty centuries of creed-making, this theologian chose and posed Jesus Christ as "the man for others." Was he abandoning and contradicting everything he had affirmed in countless sermons, class outlines, letters, and brief theological expressions? Having chosen to call into question "metaphysics," "otherworldliness," or "inwardness," was he left propagating one more in a long sequence of proposed "Jesus-centered humanisms"? If so, would it not rapidly fade, as had most of its predecessors? So the question remained urgent: who was, is, and will be Christ for the "us" about whom and to whom Bonhoeffer spoke and wrote?

The Key Issue: Continuity or Discontinuity?

The main way the scholarly world has chosen to address the problem of the earlier and the later or last Bonhoeffer was to ask whether his projections were, for all the novelties and experiments in language, substantially *continuous* with what he had stood for before his incarceration or early in his days of imprisonment, or are they *discontinuous*, and thus potentially in contradiction with the heart of what he had represented and elaborated before the final scenes in the Tegel prison years? The radical interpreters and formulators in both the European East and the modern West were emphatic: they found *discontinuity*, a clear breach. This was a discovery or a claim that, it must be said, was plausible, because some of the late Bonhoeffer writings gave signs that this second assessment may be warranted. Yet, as the years have passed, it is obvious that most of those who had known the earlier Bonhoeffer and who studied texts from "before" and "after" April 30, 1944, argue, against Hanfried Müller, Bishop Robinson, the "Christian atheists," and those who left the church behind, that there was *continuity*. Despite the provocative materials in some prison letters, Bonhoeffer's life and thinking seemed seamless if dynamic and restless.

Such an assessment did not and could not mean that there had been no important changes in his world and thought. He knew that the changes were profound, and he feared that confiding word of them could be unsettling to Bethge. Even had he not voiced misgivings about uttering word of change, it would have been almost inconceivable to picture that someone so alert to circumstances and who was so much an experimenter and explorer could have gone through what he did without significantly changing. But did this change call into question and even cancel out everything else Bonhoeffer confessed and professed? The differing answers that readers, guided by informed critics, give to those questions help shape the setting of agendas in the light of his work. They help assure a continuing life for the book in the new millennium.

"Disturbing" and even "dangerous" are words we have read in writings by Edwin Robertson, sometimes by Eberhard Bethge, and even by Reginald Fuller, his translator and early expositor in England. Fuller, like some of the others, found the probings of 1944 enigmatic and spoke of "the riddle of Bonhoeffer." Of course, lovers of mysteries and detective stories could help keep the book alive and market it and their own comments by posing enigmas and riddles. However, speaking of them in isolation from his life work without reference to theological substance would violate the sense of gravity and purpose so consistently manifest in Bonhoeffer.

To help those who had some familiarity with the subject, Fuller was choosing up, naming, and defining sides, as scholars often do on the battlefields called libraries and conferences. He described the first of the two schools, which stressed continuity, as being "ecclesiological and Christological." The other cluster, which stressed discontinuity, he called "the hermeneutical." Fuller located its focus in the writings of the influential German theologian Gerhard Ebeling along with Ronald Gregor Smith and Hanfried Müller. Fuller himself favored the continuity approach and spoke critically of the overeagerness of some theologians to seize on and isolate those provocative pages that appear late in the book. After citing some of these he wrote: "From these quotations we can see how the characteristic key words upon which our Anglo-American radical theologians have pounced, and which they have treated as natural, universal truths, were for Bonhoeffer strictly dependent upon the work of Jesus Christ, upon his incarnation, crucifixion, and ascension," which he had stressed in his earlier writings.[3]

Early on, many literate and honest scholars who were devoted to the Bonhoeffer works confessed that they were indeed troubled but still came to his defense. This meant that they had to admit how vulnerable to the radical interpreters his prison writings had left him. Already in 1966 some foresaw resulting havoc if not threatening chaos. Thus Edwin Robertson, a British broadcaster and pastor, early on noted how easily misunderstood the Bonhoeffer of the prison letters could be—and, he thought, as he was. The pastor demonstrated that he knew enough about human nature and culture and about the tendency of nominal Christians to find excuses to turn slugabed on the slightest excuse. They would simply drift from faith and church and relax in an undemanding world that has come of age. In a short but rich treatment Robertson confessed:

> There have been times during the past few years when I could have wished for . . . powers to withhold the *Letters and Papers from Prison* from publication until the other works had been read. These wonderful letters have been so misused that the influence of Bonhoeffer has more than once run out into shallow sands. So many people have thrilled to the ideas in those letters of the church being abolished or distinctive Christian standards being abandoned. So few have taken the trouble

to read the careful basis for Bonhoeffer's revolutionary ideas in his published works.[4]

Robertson even spoke of the precariousness of seeing Bonhoeffer as a personal example: "The morals of a martyr are not necessarily the best rules to live by. This simple fact has been emphasized many times during the past few years, as the new theology has given birth to the new morality." "The new morality" was the name for a version of situation-ethics that was critical of attempts to ground morality in natural or divine law as imparted in scriptures or in the longer moral tradition of the church. Ironically, Robertson himself talked, I must say, "situationally": "What was all right for a man in prison was the wrong medicine," he thought, for "a generation of students brought up in the prosperity of a welfare state."

"And so," his friendly but agonized critic went on, "Bonhoeffer is dangerous. He gives men an excuse for lax standards in their private lives and makes an irregular attender at church feel the comfort and support of a better man than himself." Robertson had to be combining personal impressions with anecdotal lore. Now, to my knowledge, none of the sociologists of religion took surveys trying to discern whether the concurrent decline in church attendance in the world Robinson knew so well could be tied to the reading of Bonhoeffer. It is impossible to measure the numbers of worshipers who followed the EXIT sign out of chapels because they had taken some of his sentences literally. Still, it is natural to ponder a cause-and-effect link. Historian of doctrine Jaroslav Pelikan once remarked to me that books by some of the Bonhoeffer interpreters amounted to raising and answering a question: "How little do I have to believe in order to advertise myself as a modern Christian?" Robertson, who knew his Bonhoeffer, was ready to say: "You have to believe very much, and believe it deeply," especially in relation to what he affirmed about Jesus Christ.

Robertson adduced statistics that one cannot certify, and treated his theme hyperbolically, but there *is* something to his observation: "There is no doubt that the letters from prison are exciting." When they appeared, it was hoped that the book would lead readers to "his more considered works. Unfortunately, that never happened." Bethge, of course, contradicted that. He looked at the marketing and review of books and found that readers became interested in various books in the Bonhoeffer canon after reading the letters. Robertson estimated that for every thousand people who have read this book, only one hundred would have read Bonhoeffer's most concentrated and prescriptive work, and "only one" would have read the theologian's earliest, heaviest works. There was more hyperbole to come: "The book caused much offence among religious people, and it was soon clear that the prime offender was Bonhoeffer." Still not lowering his voice, Robertson continued: "Not since Christ told the religious people of his day that harlots would go into the kingdom of heaven before them, had there been such a scandal!"

Robertson, pondering the riddle of the dangerous theologian, mused: "Bonhoeffer remained a good Lutheran and John Robinson is still a bishop of a very religious church." Out of charity to Anglican friends, I will postpone final judgment about the very religious Church of England. Since Bonhoeffer did not survive prison, no one can know if he would have returned to pulpit and pew in postwar Germany—though, as Robertson noted, his theology remained "basically Lutheran." And Robertson, after his cautionary words, strongly encouraged his readers to give good attention to Bonhoeffer.

Robertson needed to devote only a few pages to the prison letters to make his point, and half the space on his book's small pages is taken up with long quotations, but they were telling. One, of which we cannot be reminded too often on this point, is that famous passage, full of the questions Bonhoeffer posed to Bethge and, secondarily to readers: "What keeps gnawing at me is the question, what is Christianity, or who is Christ actually for us today?" The third theme, almost equally as famous, is the positive one, which Robertson could affirm, since it had to do with the church: "The church is her true self," Bonhoeffer wrote from prison, "when she exists for humanity." Robertson's summary, designed to rescue the church for contemporary life even as he would point out the need for drastic reforms in it, picked it up this way:

In the end, the final word about the church for Bonhoeffer is that it is *the expression of Christ in the world.* Christ is for him always the incarnate Christ. He continues so in his church. Thus the view of the church as a beleaguered fortress with the bridge up and only an occasional skirmish out to catch a few prisoners, is foreign to Bonhoeffer's idea of Christ and his church.[5]

Religion and the World That Has Come of Age

If Robertson saw responses in the form of indifference to faith and church resulting from Bonhoeffer's prison writings, Bethge, writing nine years later on the thirtieth anniversary of Bonhoeffer's death, dealt with a different kind of change, which we might call the rise of a "neoreligious" culture. What was the true situation of the "world that has come of age"? Bethge, as he traveled and read, had to admit that a surprising new climate was present in the American academies and elsewhere. This was a cultural context that Bonhoeffer in prison had not foreseen. "Religious studies," as a curricular field, Bethge noted, was attracting more attention than theology, and public attention made religion a public phenomenon far beyond Christian circles. In the fads of the new moment around 1975, Bethge observed that religion was increasingly coming to mean "expansions of consciousness and experiences of infinite-inducing 'trips.'"

At this time Paul Tillich, the serious celebrity theologian, gained notice with his very broad definitions of religion, for example, by seeing and associating it with "ultimate concern." These Tillichian accents, thought Bethge, were carrying the day, so much so that both the purely secular and the distinctively Christian agendas were being eclipsed.[6] "The Christian philosopher of religion," Bethge assessed, "has for the moment carried the day against the christocentric theologian." Somewhat regretfully, he also wrote: "The climate favors those who would gladly evade the critical claim of the phenomenon of Bonhoeffer." When he spoke of this being true "for the moment," the editor and biographer showed an awareness of cultural change. As one piece of evidence, he found significance in the revision or reversal by Harvey Cox. The Harvard professor had once been known as the prophet of *The Secular City*. But by the time Bethge made his assessment, Cox had become known as one who celebrated enthusiastic and ecstatic forms of Christianity. Bethge did not waver in his devotion to the Bonhoeffer who had been critical of religion, now when religion was increasingly being spoken of again with favor. "Nevertheless," wrote a steadfast Bethge, "even if it be granted that the matter has been badly put, the terms 'religionless Christianity' and 'nonreligious interpretation' stand for facts that cannot be swept under the rug when the vocabulary is rejected." Indeed, "these facts still confront us intact."

Bethge was fair to Cox as he quoted the Harvard theologian's comment on those words of Bonhoeffer that had introduced the debate over religionlessness. "What keeps gnawing at me is the question, what is Christianity . . . today?" Cox: "This is still a powerful passage. Just rereading it today speeds my pulse," and, "I have never rejected the core of Bonhoeffer. I never will." The popular theologian affirmed that overall Bonhoeffer was, and remained, "right in his search, mistaken only in his terminology."

In one of his most succinct elucidations, Bethge wrote that Bonhoeffer's main theme had nothing to do with the quantitative or statistical role of religion or religionlessness. He noted what has to be obvious, that "religious phenomena as such hardly had a place in Bonhoeffer's field of interest," and that the theologian had done very little research and writing on the history, sociology, or psychology of religion, disciplines, Bethge admitted, a scholar could hardly ignore in more recent times. What Bonhoeffer was after, as the context made clear to him, was not general cultural comment but, always, answers to his question, "Who is Christ actually for us today?"[7]

Taking a longer look back to gain perspective, as we also must, Bethge reported that the nonreligious interpretation had been received enthusiastically among many who were dealing with the aftermath of the Enlightenment, a phenomenon or event they could not disavow. It was engrained in their culture. At the same time, this interpretation awakened mistrust among those who thought Bonhoeffer had been overaccommodating to modernism and making too much of a compromise to the spirit of the times while blurring the biblical witness that had shaped him.

Bethge believed that Bonhoeffer's still valid critique of religion was not wholly novel; it had an ancestry. He properly credited Karl Barth for having criticized religion before Bonhoeffer did, and he observed that it was that senior Swiss theologian who had provided a matrix for Bonhoeffer's understanding. Barth's attack on religion had been designed to critique churches and "the religious" people who used religion to evade responsibility and ethical calls. More controversial was Bonhoeffer's seeing religion as a phenomenon that in his time still "unavoidably accompanies faith." He went on from there to observe that this accompaniment had been "a characteristic element of an epoch that is drawing to a close." Bonhoeffer went beyond Barth, thought Bethge. His expansion of that theologian's criticism was "breathtaking." Yet Bethge also saw a conservative dimension to his friend's work, since Bonhoeffer did not think that the transcending of religion in this sense would mean the end of *all* "piety, liturgy, prayer, and devotional life." The condemned man writing from prison did not eliminate these from his own life or think they had to be eliminated to match the "nonreligious interpretation" that he was offering. In their traditional form these simply could not serve as props for faith or ethics.

In sum, Western religion, the only kind Bonhoeffer treated, had long been expressed in what the imprisoned theologian called "inwardness" or "the inner life" (*Innerlichkeit*). This concept, he thought, led to a compartmentalization that boxed Christianity in from the vital world. In Bethge's eyes, some phenomena and events that might have propped up the church and faith in the past were no longer positive contributions. He was also not cheerful about prospects for vital faith and ethics in the face of what he called "a newly revived orthodoxy and a newly awakened pietism." These, he charged, too easily made peace with the world.

Here was the shocker in Bethge's analysis: he was concerned lest enduring or emerging cultures on the religious track he had just described might lead to a reversion to the policy of Germany in the 1930s, where and when the churches settled for "well-regulated and restrictive peace with contemporary society." The "new unpolitical or apolitical peace of the churches with contemporary society," he warned, could lead once more to catastrophic results. Cautions such as those were not quiet words to serve in a disquieting time.

"Even If There Were No God"

Additional disturbing theological and humanistic Bonhoeffer themes outlined in the late letters have prompted extensive and learned studies and responses. Some of them refer to the influence of Hegel on Bonhoeffer. One of these analyses appears in a sophisticated and thoughtful reading by Charles Marsh, who deals with another of the controversial Bonhoeffer themes that has made several appearances on our pages: Christian living *etsi deus non daretur*, "even if there were no God." That phrase, we recall, appeared in a passage of a letter in which Bonhoeffer pondered how the reconciliation of God and the world had been effected through the person and work of Christ. Only with this transaction in mind, wrote Marsh, "can we make sense of Bonhoeffer's perennially unsettling words at Tegel prison, 'Before God and with God we live without God. God lets himself be pushed out of the world on the cross.'" And then, still referring to the letters, "when God is spoken of in this way," Marsh quoted Bonhoeffer, "the godlessness of the world is not ... concealed but rather, revealed, and thus exposed to an unexpected light."[8]

Bonhoeffer's perplexing confession, notice, and question continue to haunt those who take them seriously. What could have been going through the mind of a man who was under virtual sentence of death, a condemned prisoner with less than a year to live? Was he experiencing abandonment by Christ, to whom he had devoted his intellectual and spiritual vocation? Whoever holds a copy of *Letters and Papers from Prison*, studies it in a class, discusses it in an International Bonhoeffer Congress, or hopes to find new focus in his or her own life in the light of the book is likely to recognize that he or she is encountering a truly creative imagination at work. What must it have been like for Bonhoeffer, as he paced in his small cell at

Tegel prison or as he stared at the ceiling and pondered his end? There, to a person of faith, the presence of Christ was supposed to be more vivid than was that of his guards and more constant than the visit of friends, whose comings and goings were being so strictly and cruelly monitored. The circumstances of encounter, but not the questions, are vastly different for readers.

Bonhoeffer did not leave the Christ-centered theme that he had long favored. Still, he figuratively pulled down the curtain on the stage where for twenty centuries Christ had been understood one way, "when we could tell people that with words—whether with theological or with pious words," but that time, he concluded, "is past." Then he offered a contextual theme that was becoming central to what we might call his philosophy or anthropology: what was "over," he went on, "is the age of inwardness and of conscience—and that means the age of religion altogether." Through the decades in which the book containing this sentence lives on, those lines have inspired questioning, debate, and, for some, liberation.

Peter Selby of Durham Cathedral in England picked up on the theme. We can let him stand as representative of many in the newer times. He mentioned that he was maturing in the generation that was being influenced by the previous one, which had made the "creative misuse" of Bonhoeffer to which John de Gruchy and others had referred.[9] Selby confessed that he also had been carried away with enthusiasm by Bonhoeffer's radical projections. He had rejected the conservative backlashers like one who said in a sermon "that St. Luke had pulled Dr. [John A. T.] Robinson's leg and it had come off in his hand."[10] He remembered the wild optimism among liberal interpreters in the *Honest to God* era, but he had to note that they saw their hopes for creative secularism dashed. It was replaced by a secularism that does not even ask the questions to which Bonhoeffer's testimony offered tentative solutions. On the other hand, Selby also noted the rise of Christian and other fundamentalisms "which suggest that for many the proper response of religion to modernity" is "strident confrontation." It was time to revisit Bonhoeffer, Selby thought, in efforts to transcend that polarity.[11] As he faced contemporary culture in the West, the younger man spoke of his generation: "Such is the struggle of a theologian confronted with modernity. He sees a contrast between 'old world perplexity and new world resistance.'"[12] This was a contrast made stark in the mind of Selby himself, as he watched the British churches emptying. Such emptying was not yet predominant in the South African culture where he was delivering a lecture. There, churches were prospering.

While Selby's essay is intentionally modest and preliminary, designed to frame a conference paper, he almost uncannily managed to speak for many readers of the letters in many cultures and circumstances.

He was succinct as he spoke of how the new concerns related first to *identity*: "In a world that is *mündig*, who is Jesus Christ? Is he among those who manifest their *Mündigkeit*, living *etsi deus non daretur*, as God requires, before God, without God?" All this in a culture where *religious* identity and identifiability," he noted, "can no longer be assumed." The questions now for his audience and readers were: "Who are you, Christ? Fanatic? Moralist? Market leader? Refugee? Bankrupt? And the response is the question put to us, 'Who are we?' "[13]

The second issue is signaled by the word "today" in the Bonhoeffer letter. Selby observed that it "can be read in liberal or radical mode: it may be the today of those who are sure of their own today and ask how Christ may fit into it, or it may be that 'today' is 'today' as Christ the 'humiliated God-man' sees it and asks us to see it."[14] The former concept belongs to those in power; the latter, to those "who have no voice in decisions about how our world is to be used and abused in the service of those who rule and shape what he referred to as our "today."

Admittedly, Selby contributed little to formal Christology and made no reference to centuries of debate over the substance of it, yet his essay served the purpose of drawing readers into the life of the book, and not leaving them standing at the sidelines being awed or repelled by the answers Bonhoeffer came up with, urgent as they, too, will be, and demanding of readers' energies as they are.

The Last and the Lost Letters

As puzzles and controversies over how to interpret the provocative materials in the last letters developed, Bethge had to bring up once again the sad note: readers of the book who were curious about the meanings of the provisional sketches and provocations wanted to read of the follow-up, "but these September letters," Bethge said, "were the ones I had burned in the fireplace just before my own arrest." When he first had done so, he remembered, he felt exhilarated and free. Now, given all the attention they were receiving, he was "afflicted with the tormenting afterthought," he confessed, "that I was responsible for the destruction of what may have contained decisive developments of Bonhoeffer's ideas, but developments which I can no longer recall."

As with lives, so it is with books. When someone dies, there is almost always in the minds of survivors some sense of unfinishedness, as in "if only she had spoken one more time," or "I wish I had asked, but now we'll never know." Bethge closed the door on speculation about what was in the burned letters, frustrating though their disappearance had to be to anyone looking for a finished product or some final resolution. Yet, in the spirit of conversation with a text, he offered a virtual charter for continuing engagement: "There is no longer anything from Bonhoeffer, then, that can take us beyond the theological positions of his published letters. All that is open to us is to make a careful examination of what we have in order to ascertain whether or not the hints he gives us indicate the right direction we must take in the fulfillment of our tasks."[15]

"*Our* tasks": who are the "we" and "us" in that statement? Bethge was speaking primarily to the Christian world, though I would argue that non- or anti-Christians who want to make sense of twenty-first-century Christianity will be wrestling with the issue the late Bonhoeffer raised. They will do this in some cases by conscious reference to him, or, more often, not. What he said about the "world that has come of age" provides a framework for debate over secularization and the revival of religion around the globe. What he envisioned in the category of "religion-less Christianity"[16] is an address to a scene in which inherited Christian institutions, traditions, and formulas are being radically transformed. Living as Christians in the world "even if there were no God" remains a challenge. The God-question also poses issues in a time when the Christian third of the world faces ever more challenging encounters with other religions.

Continuity: The Christological Clue

Finally, however, the issue Bonhoeffer posed to friend Bethge on April 30, 1944, is focused in the enduring, haunting, and challenging question: "Who is Christ actually for us today?" In a recent book on global

Christianity, I had to ask what seemed to be basic and continuous among Christians rich and poor, north and south, traditional and experimental, in an age of science and turmoil. I was drawn back to James D. G. Dunn's *Unity and Diversity in the New Testament*. Dunn revisited all the New Testament glimpses of what was agreed upon and what was a source of conflict among early Christians. Finally it came to him to phrase it something like "the human Jesus is the exalted Lord." So the "task" today for believer and nonbeliever alike is to ask what that means in the various cultural circumstances, as Bonhoeffer asked in his own.[17]

It should be clear that, without my suggesting that this biography of one book of letters settles or could settle the issues, my own tracing leads me to side with the scholars who find continuity in Bonhoeffer. Without taking away from the radicalism of his observations and proposals, it becomes obvious that Christology remained the central theme. It is not possible here to give this thesis a full hearing; bibliographies on the subject are enormous, and to do justice to them would be to skew the plot of this biography of one book as opposed to a full-scale analysis of the life work of a theologian. Following the self-imposed rules of the game that I set to provide some discipline to this biography, I continue to confine myself to this one book. So this is not the place to page through volume after volume of his earlier work. Instead, my question is: what was the Christological exposition *in these letters*, written at the time when he was rejecting so much of what had surrounded his life work, the culture and much theological expression of Western Christianity?

Earlier when discussing the comprehensive treatment by Ernst Feil, a Roman Catholic scholar, I put a tag and a paper clip on several pages to signal a commitment to return to pages wherein Feil dealt with the subject. His is as consistent, comprehensive, and succinct a treatment as I have found. It concurs with what Eberhard Bethge, who knew Bonhoeffer best, had also noted. Feil confronts the issue in a section on "The Question of God." "Given the circumstances, it is understandable that the question 'Who is God?' is very urgent." Citation follows citation from the late letters, all of them affirming the reality of God, but doing so in fresh ways. Thus Feil reminds us that Bonhoeffer resisted seeing God as "the working hypothesis" or "the stop-gap" or a deus ex machina.[18] He also rejected the concept of God's work as "tutelage." Never for him could divine transcendence refer only to what occurs "on the far side drawn by the boundary of death." Relying too much on the witness to God as "the Almighty" had become a problem in the new context. When Bonhoeffer asked, "Who is God?" he was not answering the question by reference to abstract belief in God, "in his omnipotence, etc. That is not a genuine experience of God, but a partial extension of the world."

Feil noted the positive point by Bonhoeffer: "I should like to speak of God not on the boundaries but at the center, not in weakness but in strength; and therefore not in death and guilt but in our life and goodness.... God is the beyond in the midst of our life." Here is where Christ, for him, came in: we know from Christ what transcendence is, thought Bonhoeffer, for he "takes hold of us at the center of our lives." So, Feil says, "For Bonhoeffer God is always 'God in Jesus Christ.' His was not the God of religion but 'the God of the Bible.'"

Here Feil and his translator Martin Rumscheidt have to clear up some grammar and translation to make the point. A most important footnote reads: "The 'death-of-God' theology really cannot claim Bonhoeffer for its foundation. Following him one can only state that we must live in this world 'even if God *were* dead." An early Catholic commentator, William Kuhns got it wrong when he translated the Latin *etsi deus non daretur* as "to which God is not given." Kuhns, say these commentators, must have assumed that Bonhoeffer's statement is in the indicative. The 1962 edition had caused the trouble because, notes Feil, it "deletes Bonhoeffer's conjunctival translation, 'even if there were no God.'" More recent and accurate translations have restored the phrase.[19]

Where are you taking us? I can picture a reader asking. We were minding our business and suddenly we are faced with a Latin grammar lesson. Feil again: "What is significant is that we must live in this world *etsi deus non daretur*," "even if there were no God." "What must not be overlooked is that Bonhoeffer made use of a formulation in the conjunctive; it occurred first in the discussion of Hugo Grotius's teaching on natural law and was used again, but in order to generalize a point. To change the conjunctive into the indicative is to distort the statements of Bonhoeffer!"

One of the last surviving letters makes clear that Bonhoeffer "derived true knowledge of God from the earthly Jesus, the historical Jesus Christ." His letter quoted Paul's First Letter to the Corinthians 1:20: "He is the 'Yes' pronounced upon God's promises, every one of them. That is why, when we give glory to God, it is through Christ Jesus that we say 'Amen.'" The key to everything for Bonhoeffer was the "in him." Coming down to earth: "But the truth is that if this earth was good enough for the man Jesus Christ, if such a man as Jesus lived, then, and only then has life a meaning for us." Suddenly, as Feil expounded in these letters, transcendence has become not a matter of "distance" or "beyondness," but of "closeness." So "Christ is no longer an object of religion, but something quite different, really the Lord of the world."[20]

It is this drastic change in the concept of transcendence that led Bonhoeffer to turn more and more to the Old Testament, the Hebrew Bible. It was no longer for him a document to be read as a preparation for Jesus Christ, but as the advocate of "profound this-worldliness." What was this about being restrained in talking about concepts of God? From his reading in prison Bonhoeffer came to a fresh awareness that "it is only when one knows the unutterability of the name of God that one can utter the name of Jesus Christ."

To show how far "thisworldliness" took him, he wrote to friend Bethge, he was rereading the Song of Songs, which had been long treated allegorically for Christian consumption. No, he advised: take it straight. It is an "ordinary love song," which is "probably the best 'christological exposition.'"[21]

For Bonhoeffer the accent on Jesus as "the man for others" in whom God is encountered in the midst of the world did not mean that the author was a Christomonist. This means that he was not someone who reduced the Divine Trinity to Jesus the Son as its "Second Person," leaving out the Father and the Holy Spirit. Feil ended his own attempt to do justice to Bonhoeffer's witness by summarizing: "a christocentric theology for him was the attempt to speak of the mystery, something we can only do in contradictions and paradoxes."[22]

Bonhoeffer could live with both contradictions and paradoxes, and he did so through his *Letters and Papers from Prison*. That feature, among all the other attractions, elicited the variety of responses to the book that have assured for it a life long enough already to warrant its being called a classic, a book to be used as a means of interpreting events.

Sending the Book Further along Its Way

As I release this book into the bibliographical and biographical stream, I should step forward and declare myself on some of the main themes. Up to this point I have tried to stand at the sidelines, observing and reporting on a sampling of writings by those who did their own interpreting. Here are a few declarations:

- Reading about *Letters and Papers from Prison* is no substitute for reading *Letters and Papers from Prison*, for the immediacy the life of the book manifests.
- Tracing the life of the book is no substitute for tracing the life, through any number of biographies, but beginning and ending with Eberhard Bethge's—yes—classic!
- Isolating and concentrating on the life of one book is a bid for readers to reach along the Bonhoeffer bookshelf to read pages whose topics I had to exclude from this assessment. Every one of his books will bring fresh instruments for interpreting the life revealed in this one book.
- Tempted to quote the quotable Dietrich Bonhoeffer to illustrate all points or to introduce new ones, I had to resist it. Be assured that there are scores of scenes, episodes, or meditations that had to go unquoted here but are eminently readable and memorable.
- It is clear that the concepts of "the world that has come of age," "religionless Christianity," "before God and with God we live without God," and Jesus Christ as "the man for others," and always the question "Who is Christ actually for us

today?" were the most provocative concepts inviting interpretation.

- For me, "the world that has come of age" is a historical judgment of great resonance in the parts of the world that were most immediate to Bonhoeffer, but anyone with a global vision will find evidence that it was off the mark in a world in which both "the secular" and "the religious" increase in power. It is not "a religionless world" and is not becoming one. But Bonhoeffer's reflections on the emergent secularity that he saw are of great import to those who want to relate religion and faith to the secular that he observed so astutely.

- Living "before God and with God without God" and living *etsi deus non daretur* are provocative ways to pose fresh understandings of God in a new time.

- "The man for others" does not do justice to many classical and enduring themes that Christians associate with the Trinity and Jesus Christ, but the phrase strips away many obscuring forms of witness and makes it possible for believers to undertake new ethical missions.

Bonhoeffer's effort to pare away irrelevancies in the community or the institutional life of faith was unnecessary for those who actively or passively walk away from the church in its many forms and does not serve well the interests he did promote for the acts of justice and mercy, or identification with humans who have nothing to do with Christ.

The fact that the strongest clue for interpreting Bonhoeffer, according to most serious students, is Christology will make it difficult for those who would hold the interest of, among others, Jews, Muslims, Hindus, Buddhists, secularists, and more, among whom Jesus "the man for others" seems distant, irrelevant, or destructive. Yet there is much for them, in this age of interactions among the faiths and with nonfaith, in the efforts for Christians who in each generation have to ask anew, "Who is Christ actually for us today?"

Had we had the final letters, which were burned, we would not likely find in them ways out of the enigmas or to resolve the paradoxes of Bonhoeffer's still "dangerous" and creative ponderings and proposals. Bethge had read them before he had to burn them, and he recalled nothing that would be determinative for interpreting the Bonhoeffer we already have, or the book whose life we have traced. Interpreting Bonhoeffer can issue in an argument without end or, better, a conversation with ever new beginnings.

Naming a Strategy: "The Arcane Discipline"

Among the many leftover issues on which Bonhoeffer wrote too little and to which Bonhoeffer scholars devote themselves, some would say too much, are those that have to do with an apparent paradox in his life unto its end. He spoke so strongly about Jesus "the man for others" when he dealt with ethics, including the ethics of resistance, and so critically of religion and piety as he knew them, that he seemed to down-value worship and prayer. Yet he devoted himself through the prison years to prayer and went to the gallows still observed as a man of prayer. Was this adult Christian in an adult world regressing to immaturity and running back for refuge to prayer? Was he abandoning his life work, which was profoundly concerned with community, a concern he carried through *Letters and Papers from Prison?* Was he inconsistent, a turncoat's turncoat who turned from worship but then, when everything became urgent, turned back to it and prayed with and for others?

Questions like this have drawn the energies of the people I think of as my own generation, some would say "mainstream Protestants and Catholics" who have not been sidetracked and now abandoned with the Marxist or "honest to God" or "death of God" interpreters *or* taken the path of reaction against them all in new fundamentalisms. What strikes one in the most recent decades is the way this mainstream generation has returned to the issue of worship, community life, and prayer. People who have been mentors among us in these years—Americans Larry Rasmussen, Burton Nelson, Geffrey Kelly, or, across the Atlantic, Keith Clements and so many more—have picked through the letters and found too-brief comments that provide clues to the Bonhoeffer who wrote so much about community and worship.

None of them, to my knowledge, has domesticated Bonhoeffer, smoothed his rough edges or come up with safe theologies of their own. Here is an instance: in a couple of paragraphs in the letters he advocated that the church seek new patterns of communication—including silence!—new postures—including diffidence—and new forms, including the arcane discipline, *disciplina arcani*. The reader legitimately asks for a pause and for explanation. From where did that term come and what does it mean? Through the years Larry Rasmussen has wrestled with this, picking up from Bonhoeffer's line that "people as they are now simply cannot be religious anymore." This opened the question of worship, which Bonhoeffer himself took up: "The questions to be answered [about worship] surely would be: 'What do a church, a community, a sermon, a liturgy, a Christian life mean in a religionless world?' [and] 'What is the place of worship and prayer in a religionless situation?' Does the secret discipline . . . take on a new importance here?"[23]

Rasmussen knows he has to explain the arcane discipline, a phrase picked up from early Christianity, but he did so by referring to what it was not, in the culture of religious America: "Worship as arcane discipline is not for the streets, the posters, or the mass media. It is certainly not Hollywood Bowl and drive-in Easter sunrise services or Sunday East Room exercises in American civil religion in the White House, nor Astrodome rallies of religiosity. It is not bumper-sticker and slick paper Christianity." What it is comes out in little snatches from Rasmussen: the arcane discipline is "the focused inner concentration," or "the hidden discipline of intense nurture and disciplined worship of small groups of strongly committed Christians who make up the church as a kind of low-profile Christian order in the world come of age. . . . It means groups of Christians operating rather incognito in the world, making common cause with the non-Christian and the nonreligious."

Geffrey B. Kelly, another longtime participant in Bonhoeffer studies, pointed to two other Bonhoeffer scholars who elaborated on themes from the letters. One, Paul Lehmann, a friend of Bonhoeffer's, noted that Bonhoeffer "was convinced that a community of faith practicing the *Arkandisziplin* was needed to prevent Christians from losing their Christlike identity in the midst of their solidarity with the 'world-come-of-age.' It was essential, but to remain a secret affair, not to be brandished triumphantly before or forced upon an unwilling world." And Kelly drew on Oskar Hammelsbeck for another paraphrase of lines in the letters: "Christ's remaining with us and our remaining by Christ delivers us from all stagnation in religious forms. Our bond with Christ is arcane, in that even though we may be chosen and favored, we don't make this a matter of privilege or of a religiously separate existence. It is part of this *arcanum* that I hold to preaching, baptism and the eucharist, that I worship, confess and give praise within the community."[24]

John W. Matthews has provided one of the most helpful pathways to and through Bonhoeffer's somewhat confusing introduction of the terms *arkandisziplin* and *disciplina arcani*. In these late letters, says Matthews, the term implies the "'responsible sharing of the mystery' of Christian faith also in the context of the secular community through prayer, righteous action, qualified silence, and the nonreligious interpretation of biblical concepts in a world come of age. Bonhoeffer's rather "casual" use of the terms, argues Matthews, prompted misinterpretations by "enthusiasts" who welcomed his "'secret discipline' as a pious counterpart to the worldly non-religious, secular interpretation of biblical concepts." In a footnote Matthews elaborates: "*Disciplina arcani* represents significantly more than an inward, private, devotional counterpart to an outward, public, ethical non-religious interpretation of biblical concepts." Bonhoeffer with this term provided a feast for those who wanted to develop his own provocative and sketchy probes and suggestions.[25]

Beyond the Book: The Last Days of the Author

Finally, I picture that many who have been introduced to the life of the man through the book made up of his writings will have one object of curiosity that will prevail over all others. While I have steadfastly restricted this tracing of the life of the book, whose biography it is, I was thus unable to deal with the last days and the death of the author. Bethge's notes in the standard edition that was before us did not detail that conclusion. Just this once, I will cheat and introduce some post–*Letters and Papers from Prison* narrative.

The story has often been told: In January 1945 Bonhoeffer still asked his parents to send books so he could study, and he remained busy with theological work, as if he had years ahead of him. He was interrogated and evidently did what he could to confuse the officials who were trying to learn more about him and his colleagues' opinions and work. On February 7 he was moved to Buchenwald, near Weimar, where he was given a basement cell. British Captain Payne Best, a fellow prisoner but a survivor and author of a book about those days, *The Venlo Incident*, reported and included this assessment of Bonhoeffer: "Bonhoeffer was all humility and sweetness; he always seemed to diffuse an atmosphere of happiness, of joy in every smallest event in life, and of deep gratitude for the mere fact of being alive. There was something dog-like in the look of fidelity in his eyes and his gladness if you showed that you liked him. He was one of the very few men I ever met to whom his God was real and ever close to him.[26]

Resisting the impulse to turn this into a biography of the author and not the book, I will move expeditiously. Best, again, reporting on Bonhoeffer the morning before his death at Flossenbürg, a site for executions: "He spoke about the thoughts and decisions this captivity had produced in everyone. After this service the other prisoners wanted to smuggle Bonhoeffer over to their room so that he could hold a service there also. But it was not long before the door was opened and two civilians called out: 'Prisoner Bonhoeffer, get ready and come with us!' "[27]

A collection of fellow prisoners survived as witnesses. Bonhoeffer was especially eager that Best get a posthumous message to Bishop Bell of Chichester, who had served as a liaison to Bonhoeffer and his colleagues in the last years. Bethge, who reported on these last hours, quoted a camp doctor, who did not know who Bonhoeffer was but remembered him well in a memoir written ten years after the event: "I was most deeply moved by the way this lovable man prayed, so devout and so certain that God heard his prayer. At the place of execution, he again said a short prayer and then climbed the steps to the gallows, brave and composed. His death ensued after a few seconds. In the almost fifty years that I worked as a doctor, I have hardly ever seen a man die so entirely subject to the will of God."[28] He left these last words, in Best's hearing and version: "This is the end—for me the beginning of life."

CHAPTER 1   The Beginning

1. Eberhard Bethge, *Dietrich Bonhoeffer: A Biography.
   Theologian, Christian, Man for His Times,* rev. and
   ed. Victoria J. Barnett (Minneapolis: Fortress Press,
   2000), 832f, discusses Bonhoeffer's references to possible suicide.

2. Dietrich Bonhoeffer, *Letters and Papers from Prison:
   The Enlarged Edition* (New York: Touchstone Edition, 1997), hereafter cited as LPP. Its full original title
   was Dietrich Bonhoeffer, *Widerstand und Ergebung:
   Briefe und Aufzeichnungen aus der Haft* Herausgege-
   ben von Christian Gremmels, Eberhard Bethge und
   Renate Bethge in Zusammenarbeit mit Ilse Tödt
   (Gütersloh: Chr. Kaiser Verlag, 1998) (Dietrich Bonhoeffer Werke Band 8). The definitive English edition, which I will normally cite, includes many names
   of editors and translators. I will list them here, both
   out of respect for their labors and to indicate something of the complexity of the project that grew out of
   the messages that issued from Tegel Prison: Dietrich

Bonhoeffer, *Letters and Papers from Prison*, trans. from the German edition, ed. Christian Gremmels, Eberhard Bethge, and Renate Bethge, with Ilse Tödt; English edition ed. John W. de Gruchy, trans. Isabel Best, Lisa Dahill, Reinhard Krauss, and Nancy Lukens; "After Ten Years" trans. Barbara and Martin Rumscheidt; supplementary material trans. Douglas W. Stott (Minneapolis: Fortress Press, 2010). Following standard procedure, below I shorten the reference to DBWE 8.

3. LPP 128f, DBWE 8:180f. The German original and LPP have *consolatio fratrum;* *DBWE* translates the first word, *consolation.*

4. Ibid.

5. LPP 176; DBWE 8:238.

6. LPP 128–131; DBWE 8:181–183.

7. LPP 171; DBWE 8:232f.

8. LPP 171, 41ff; DBWE 8:82–87.

9. LPP 21f, DBWE 8:56f.

10. LPP 25; DBWE 8:60.

11. Dietrich Bonhoeffer, *Prisoner for God: Letters and Papers from Prison*, ed. Eberhard Bethge, trans. Reginald H. Fuller (New York: Macmillan, 1953).

12. Karl Barth, *Der Römerbrief,* 1st ed. (Berne: G. A. Bäschlin, 1919). The second edition, which became standard, was translated as *The Epistle to the Romans* (New York: Oxford, 1935).

13. David Tracy, *Plurality and Ambiguity: Hermeneutics, Religion, Hope* (New York: Harper and Row, 1987), 12.

14. Ibid., 19.

15. Ibid.

16. Report of the Commission on the Humanities, *The Humanities in American Life* (Berkeley: University of California Press, 1980), 1.

17. Stephen R. Haynes, *The Bonhoeffer Phenomenon: Portraits of a Protestant Saint* (Minneapolis: Fortress, 2004). I acknowledge a debt to the author of this commendable review of literature and comment on the Bonhoeffer corpus.

CHAPTER 2 The "Gradual" Editor

1. LPP viii.

2. Eberhard Bethge, "The Editing and Publishing of the Bonhoeffer Papers," *Andover Newton Bulletin*, vol. 52, no. 2 (December 1959): 1–5.

3. Ibid.

4. LPP 217; DBWE 8:303: "Ich habe mir hier oft Gedanken darüber gemacht, wo die Grenzen zwischen dem notwendigen Widerstand gegen das 'Schicksal' und der ebenso notwendigen Ergebung liegen."

5. LPP 392; DBWE 8:516f.

6. LPP 383; DBWE 8:518.

7. Ruth-Alice von Bismarck and Ulrich Kabitz, *Love Letters from Cell 92: The Correspondence between Dietrich Bonhoeffer and Maria von Wedemeyer, 1943–45*, trans. John Brownjohn (Nashville: Abingdon, 1994).

8. LPP 384ff; DBWE 8:507.

9. LPP 145; DBWE 8:200; a letter of November 26, 1943.

10. Martin E. Marty, *The Place of Bonhoeffer: Essays on the Problems and Possibilities in His Thought* (New York: Association Press, 1962). The theologians, whose work continued for four decades, included Peter

Berger, George Forell, Reginald Fuller, Walter Harrelson, Franklin Littell, Jaroslav Pelikan, and Franklin Sherman.

11. Ronald Gregor Smith, ed., *World Come of Age* (Philadelphia: Fortress, 1967).

CHAPTER 3   The Decisive Turns

1. LPP 16; DBWE 8:52.

2. LPP 27; DWBE 8:64.

3. *Widerstand und Ergebung*, 402.

4. LPP 279; DBWE 8:362.

5. LPP 280; DBWE 8:362f.

6. LPP 341; DBWE 8:450.

7. LPP 360; DBWE 8:478.

8. Ibid.

9. LPP 348f; DBWE 8:460f.

10. Ibid.; John Mathews, *Anxious Souls Will Ask: The Christ-Centered Spirituality of Dietrich Bonhoeffer* (Minneapolis: Fortress, 2005).

11. Ralf K. Wüstenberg, *A Theology of Life: Dietrich Bonhoeffer's Religionless Christianity*, trans. Doug Stott (Grand Rapids, MI: Eerdmans, 1998), xiv. This book contains one of the most sustained discussions of the influence of Dilthey and Ortega on Bonhoeffer's new proposals; see the extended illuminating comment, on which I have drawn, pp. 100–145.

12. John W. De Gruchy, ed., *Bonhoeffer for a New Day: Theology in a Time of Transition* (Grand Rapids, MI: Eerdmans, 1997).

13. Ibid., 57.

14. In Wilhelm Dilthey, *Gesammelte Schriften Bd. II, 7* (Stuttgart/Göttingen, 1964).

15. Ernst Feil, *The Theology of Dietrich Bonhoeffer*, trans. Martin Rumscheidt (Philadelphia: Fortress, 1985), 178ff.

16. LPP 326; DBWE 8:426.

17. Wüstenberg in *Bonhoeffer for a New Day*, ed. de Gruchy, 70.

CHAPTER 4 Travels East

1. Eberhard Bethge, *Bonhoeffer: Exile and Martyr*, ed. John W. de Gruchy (New York: Seabury, 1970), 24.

2. Hanfried Müller, *Von der Kirche zur Welt: Ein beitrag zu der Beziehung des Wortes Gottes auf die societas in Dietrich Bonhoeffers theologischer Entwicklung* (Leipzig: Koehler & Amelang, 1961).

3. John Godsey, *The Theology of Dietrich Bonhoeffer* (Philadelphia: Westminster, 1960).

4. Bethge, *Bonhoeffer: Exile and Martyr*, 18, 19, 23.

5. Ibid., 23.

6. John W. de Gruchy, *Daring, Trusting Spirit: Bonhoeffer's Friend Eberhard Bethge* (Minneapolis: Fortress, 2005), 131.

7. Ibid.

8. Albrecht Schoenherr's reflection appeared in *The Christian Century*, November 27, 1985, and is accessible through the magazine's website, http://www.christiancentury.org.

9. Robert F. Goeckel, *The Lutheran Church and the East German State: Political Conflict and Change under Ulbricht and Honecker* (Ithaca: Cornell University Press, 1990).

10. Hanfried Müller, "Concerning the Reception and Interpretation of Bonhoeffer," in Ronald Gregor Smith, *World Come of Age,* 210.

11. Karl Barth and Johannes Hamel, *How to Serve God in a Marxist Land* (New York: Association Press, 1959).

12. Gerhard Winter, "Dietrich Bonhoeffer—Kämpfer gegen Krieg and Faschismus," in Beiträge zur Geschichte der Humboldt-Universität zu Berlin 5 1981) Seite 5, quoted by John A. Moses, "Bonhoeffer's Reception in East Germany," in *Bonhoeffer for a New Day*, ed. de Gruchy, 282.

13. Moses, "Bonhoeffer's Reception in East Germany," 281, 285.

14. Hanfried Müller, "Concerning the Reception and Interpretation of Dietrich Bonhoeffer," in *World Come of Age*, ed. Smith, 18.

15. Ibid., 12.

16. Ibid., 183.

17. Ibid.

18. Ibid., 186.

19. Ibid., 187–188. Italics mine.

20. Ibid., 189.

21. Ibid., 191.

CHAPTER 5 Travels West

1. Alasdair MacIntyre, *Against the Self-Images of the Age: Essays on Ideology and Philosophy* (London: Duckworth, 1971), 22.

2. Reginald Fuller, ed., *Two Studies in the Theology of Bonhoeffer by Jürgen Moltmann and Jürgen Weissbach* (New York: Scribner's, 1967), 11.

3. Ibid., 12. References are also to LPP 168, 209, 237–239; DBWE 8:364, 373, on Barth.

4. John W. de Gruchy, *Confessions of a Christian Humanist* (Minneapolis: Fortress, 2006), 81–84,

discusses de Gruchy's encounters with Bonhoeffer and Robinson.

5. Bethge, *Bonhoeffer: Exile and Martyr*, 11–25, gives an account of responses and makes his own.

6. Jürgen Moltmann and Jürgen Weissbach, *Two Studies in the Theology of Bonhoeffer*, trans. Reginald H. Fuller and Ilse Fuller (New York: Scribner's, 1967), 13.

7. Georg Huntemann, *The Other Bonhoeffer: An Evangelical Reassessment of Dietrich Bonhoeffer*, trans. Todd Huizinga (Grand Rapids, MI: Baker Books, 1993), 63.

8. Harvey Cox, *The Secular City* (New York: Macmillan, 1965).

9. André Dumas, *Dietrich Bonhoeffer: Theologian of Reality*, trans. Robert McAfee Brown (New York: Macmillan: 1968), 254, n. 23.

10. For samples of this literature, see Gabriel Vahanian, *The Death of God: The Culture of Our Post-Christian Era* (New York: Braziller, 1961); Thomas J. J Altizer and William Hamilton, *Radical Theology and the Death of God* (Indianapolis: Bobbs-Merrill, 1966); Paul Van Buren, *The Secular Meaning of the Gospel* (New York: Macmillan, 1963).

11. William Hamilton, "'The Letters Are a Particular Thorn': Some Themes in Bonhoeffer's Prison Writings," in *World Come of Age*, ed. Smith, 131.

12. In Altizer and Hamilton, *Radical Theology*, 37.

13. Ibid., 39f.

14. Ibid., 42.

15. Ibid., 93.

16. Ibid., 114; see the whole essay from *The Nation*, in ibid., 113–118.

17. Paul L. Lehmann, "Faith and Worldliness in Bonhoeffer's Thought," *Union Seminary Quarterly Review*, vol. 23, no. 1 (Fall 1967): 34.

18. Bethge, *Bonhoeffer: Exile and Martyr*, 24.

CHAPTER 6 The Worlds of Two Strangers

1. Ibid., 25.

2. Heinrich Ott, *Reality and Faith: The Theological Legacy of Dietrich Bonhoeffer* (Philadelphia: Fortress, 1972); the first German edition was dated 1966.

3. Ibid., 28, 62, quoting LPP 382; DBWE 8:502. The apparently strange syntax, "wrong question," is explained by the fact that this was shorthand in Bonhoeffer's rough draft of an outline for a book.

4. Bethge, *Bonhoeffer: Exile and Martyr*, 25.

5. LPP 40; DBWE 8:81.

6. LPP 135f; DBWE 8:189.

7. LPP 214; DBWE 8:298.

8. LPP 216; DBWE 8:302f.

9. LPP 231f; DBWE 8:322f.

10. LPP 401; DBWE 8:552.

11. LPP 369; DBWE 8:486.

12. Kenneth Woodward, *Making Saints: How the Catholic Church Determines Who Becomes a Saint, Who Doesn't, and Why* (New York: Simon and Schuster 1996).

13. Lawrence S. Cunningham, *The Meaning of Saints* (San Francisco: Harper and Row, 1980), 173, 167–168.

14. René Marlé, *Bonhoeffer: The Man and His Work*, trans. Rosemary Sheed (Glen Rock, NJ: Newman, 1968), 9f.

15. Ibid., 120f.

16. Ibid., 140.

17. Ibid., 17.

18. Feil, *The Theology of Dietrich Bonhoeffer*, xv. The introduction speaks of this as "later season" work on Bonhoeffer and includes important comment on Bonhoeffer translations.

19. Ibid., xix.

20. Ibid., xxf.

21. Ibid., 4.

22. Julius Rieger, "Contacts with London," in *I Knew Dietrich Bonhoeffer*, ed. Wolf-Dieter Zimmermann and Ronald Gregor Smith (New York: Harper and Row, 1966), 96; for the comment about the temptation to turn Catholic, see Feil, *The Theology of Dietrich Bonhoeffer*, 26.

23. From George M. Marsden, "The Evangelical Denomination," in *Evangelicalism and Modern America* (Grand Rapids, MI: Eerdmans, 1984), vii–ix; see Alister McGrath, *Evangelicalism & the Future of Christianity* (Downers Grove, IL: Intervarsity, 1995), 197.

24. Stephen R. Haynes, "Between Fundamentalism and Secularism: The American Evangelical Love Affair with Dietrich Bonhoeffer," in *Dietrich Bonhoeffers Theologie heute: Ein Weg zwischen Fundamentalismus und Säkularismus? Dietrich Bonhoeffer's Theology Today: A Way between Fundamentalism and Secularism?*, ed. John W. de Gruchy, Stephen Plant, and Christiane Tietz (Gütersloh: Gütersloher Verlagshaus, 2009), 201–226. See also Eric Metaxas, *Dietrich Bonhoeffer: Pastor, Martyr, Prophet, Spy* (Nashville: Thomas Nelson, 2010).

25. Ibid., 201–202.

26. Ibid., 202–216.

27. Ibid., 221.

28. Ibid., 225–226.

29. Huntemann, *The Other Bonhoeffer*, 9.

30. Ibid., 11.

31. Ibid, 155.

32. Ibid, 11f.

33. Ibid., 12.

34. Ibid.

35. Ibid., 30–31.

CHAPTER 7 Travels around the World

1. This story is told by De Gruchy in *Daring, Trusting Spirit*, 109–110.

2. Bethge, *Dietrich Bonhoeffer*, 834.

3. Ibid.

4. LPP 342; DBWE 8:452.

5. De Gruchy, *Daring, Trusting Spirit*, 127.

6. John De Gruchy, *Bonhoeffer and South Africa: Theology in Dialogue* (Grand Rapids, MI: Eerdmans, 1984), 4.

7. De Gruchy, *Bonhoeffer for a New Day*, 1.

8. Ibid., 3.

9. Ibid., 365.

10. In Guy Carter, René van Eyden, Hans-Dirk van Hoogstraten, and Jurjen Wiersma, eds., *Bonhoeffer's Ethics: Old Europe and New Frontiers* (Kampen: Kok Pharos, 1991), 21–29, quoted in Haynes, *The Bonhoeffer Phenomenon*, 50–51.

11. Botman's report, which includes these questions, is in de Gruchy, *Bonhoeffer for a New Day*, 366–372.

12. Ibid., 370–372.

13. Ibid., 167, quoting LPP 361; DBWE 8:480.

14. Ivan Petrella, *Beyond Liberation Theology: A Polemic* (London: SCM Press, 2008), 125.

15. Ibid., 126–128.

16. Chung Hyun Kyung, "Dear Dietrich Bonhoeffer: A Letter," in *Bonhoeffer for a New Day*, ed. de Gruchy, 9–19.

17. Josiah Ulysses Young III, *No Difference in the Fare: Dietrich Bonhoeffer and the Problem of Racism* (Grand Rapids, MI: Eerdmans, 1998).

18. Thomas Day, in a Ph.D. dissertation quoted in ibid., 1.

19. Ibid., 2.

20. Ibid., 4.

21. Ibid., 1–4.

22. Ibid., 6.

23. Ibid., 163, 167; see LPP 360–361; DBWE 8:480.

24. Young, *No Difference in the Fare*, 167; see also Feil, *The Theology of Dietrich Bonhoeffer*, 199.

25. Young, *No Difference in the Fare*, 2f, quoting a phrase of Bonhoeffer scholar André Dumas.

26. Ibid., 4f.

27. Ibid., 168, quoting Feil, *The Theology of Dietrich Bonhoeffer*, 199.

28. Ibid., 171.

CHAPTER 8 Continuity and Change

1. LPP 279; DBWE 8:362.

2. *International Bulletin of Missionary Research*, vol. 34, no. 1 (January 2009): 36.

3. Fuller, *Two Studies in the Theology of Bonhoeffer*, 15f.

4. E. H. Robertson, *Dietrich Bonhoeffer* (Richmond: John Knox, 1966). See pp. vii–ix for the following quotations from Robertson.

5. Ibid., 34.

6. Eberhard Bethge, "Bonhoeffer's Assertion of Religionless Christianity—Was He Mistaken?" in *A Bonhoeffer Legacy: Essays in Understanding*, ed. A. J. Klassen (Grand Rapids, MI: Eerdmans, 1981). All the quotations here from Bethge are in a short essay, pp. 3–11.

7. Bethge is quoting Cox, *The Seduction of the Spirit*, 141, 126–128, 221.

8. Charles Marsh, *Reclaiming Dietrich Bonhoeffer: The Promise of His Theology* (New York: Oxford University Press, 1994), 164, n. 95, quoting LPP 279; DBWE 8:362.

9. John de Gruchy, ed., *Dietrich Bonhoeffer: Witness to Jesus Christ* (London: Collins, 1988), 36.

10. "Peter Selby, "Who Is Jesus Christ for Us, Today" in *Bonhoeffer for a New Day*, ed. de Gruchy, 23.

11. Ibid., 25.

12. Ibid., 23.

13. Ibid., 28.

14. Ibid., 31.

15. Bethge, "The Editing and Publishing of the Bonhoeffer Papers," 4.

16. LPP 280–282; DBWE 8:362–364, is an elaboration of the idea of "religionless Christianity."

17. James D. G. Dunn, *Unity and Diversity in the New Testament: An Inquiry into the Character of Earliest Christianity* (Philadelphia: Westminster, 1977), 50–59.

18. Feil, *The Theology of Dietrich Bonhoeffer*, 90.

19. Ibid., 220, n. 71.

20. Ibid., 92.

21. Ibid., 91–99; see LPP 157, quoted here, but see also DBWE 8:213.

22. Feil, *The Theology of Dietrich Bonhoeffer*, 94–96.

23. Larry Rasmussen with Renate Bethge, *Dietrich Bonhoeffer—His Significance for North Americans* (Minneapolis: Fortress, 1990), 57ff, 68f.

24. Geffrey B. Kelly, *Liberating Faith: Bonhoeffer's Message for Today* (Minneapolis: Augsburg, 1984), 136f; see LPP 281; DBWE 8:364f, LPP 286; DBWE 8:389f. These two quotations are virtual paraphrases of or elaborations upon two other Bonhoeffer scholars, Paul Lehmann and Oskar Hammelsbeck.

25. John W. Matthews, "Responsible Sharing of the Mystery of Christian Faith: *Disciplina Arcani* in the Life and Theology of Dietrich Bonhoefferi," *Dialog*, vol. 25, no. 1: 19–25.

26. S. Payne Best, *The Venlo Incident* (London: Hutchinson, 1950), 171ff.

27. Bethge, *Dietrich Bonhoeffer*, 927.

28. H. Fischer-Hüllstrung, "A Report from Flossenbürg," in *I Knew Dietrich Bonhoeffer*, ed. Zimmermann and Smith, 232.

Barth, Karl (*cont.*)
213; religious criticism of,
225; theology of, 112
Bell, George, 246
Berdyaev, Nicolai, 182
Berlin, East Germany, 103
Berlin-Brandenburg regional
church, 85
Berlin Wall, 68, 81, 88, 95, 101,
102, 104
Berryhill, Elizabeth, *The Cup
of Trembling,* 179
Best, Payne, *The Venlo Incident,* 245–46
Bethel, West Germany,
78, 103
Bethge, Eberhard, 17, 76, 135;
in *Abwehr,* 44–45; and
Alden-Tuthill Lectures, 47;
arrest of, 32, 34; and Boesak, 196; and Catholicism,
139–41; and change in DB,
216; on confusion concerning DB's ideas, 130–31; and
Cox, 223; on creative misuse of DB, 117, 131, 133; and
DB's *Ethics,* 33; DB's last
letters destroyed by, 32–34,
73, 130, 231–32, 240; as
DB's pastor, 6; *Dietrich
Bonhoeffer,* 22, 44, 238; and
draft and military service,
10, 37, 39, 44–45; editing
by, 3–4, 5, 7, 12, 28, 31–36,
39–40, 41, 43, 45–46, 187;

education of, 37; engagement of, 7; and Feil, 152; at
Finkenwalde, 37–38; and
first publication, 42–43;
and genre questions, 43,
191; and Gossner Mission,
9; at Harvard in 1957–58,
32; and Huntemann, 173;
and interpretation of DB,
46; in London, 44; marriage of, 7, 8; motives for
lectures, 123; and Müller,
77, 78, 82, 95; and neoreligious culture, 222; on Ott,
133–34; and popularity of
DB's canon, 220; and postwar prosecution of Nazis,
187; relationship with DB,
8, 9, 37–38, 45–46; and religionless Christianity,
223–26; on responses to
DB as dangerous, 49, 50;
and Robinson, 116, 117; and
sense of seeing, 42, 45–46;
and Tillich, 223; at Union
Theological Seminary, 43–
44; in United States, 47;
visit to DB in prison, 11;
visit to Vatican, 139, 140
Bethge, Renate, 7, 47, 191
Bible, 193, 225; DB's reading of,
54; and Evangelicalism, 159;
and freedom, 205; and Fundamentalism, 158; and slavery in New Testament, 206

letter of June 30, 1944, 72, 190; letter of August 23, 1944, 176; letter of September 30, 1944, 11; letter of December 28, 1944, 17, 144; letter of January 17, 1945, 144; message (written for three friends) of Christmas, 1942, 56

Bonhoeffer, Dietrich: themes: *acedia,* 6; anxious soul, 64; arcane discipline, 242–44; "Are we still of any use?", 56, 212; "Before God and with God, we live without God," 62, 227, 238–39; betrayal and faithfulness, 52; captivity and freedom, 52; Christian as participating in sufferings of God in secular life, 72, 129, 200, 208; church as for others, 87, 202; church as true self when she exists for humanity, 221; conscience, 6–7, 57, 228; God as working hypothesis, 61, 62, 71, 234; God hypothesis, 61, 171; history, 70–71; humans as "coming of age," 171; inwardness/inner life, 57, 59, 60, 71, 215, 225–26, 228; isolation and community, 52; Jesus Christ as "the man for others," 64, 65, 86–87, 117, 151, 159, 203, 215, 237, 238–39, 240, 241; Jesus Christ helps by weakness and suffering, 62; live *etsi deus non daretur,* "even if there were no God," 61–62, 64–65, 71–72, 125, 159, 214, 227–30, 232, 235–36, 239; metaphysics, 59, 60, 65, 71, 183, 215; nonreligious interpretation of Christianity, 125; nonreligious interpretations of faith, 67; "the powerlessness of God," 171; reason, 70, 71; religionless Christianity, 58–59, 60, 65–68, 100, 102, 111, 113, 129, 151, 153–54, 159, 160, 183, 202, 223–26, 232, 238–39; religionlessness, 57–59, 69, 71, 122, 125–26, 174, 199, 200; resistance and submission *(Widerstand und Ergebung),* 40, 41, 87; suffering, 52–56, 204; *tristitia,* 6, 7; "What is Christianity?", 57, 212, 221, 224; "Who are we?", 230; "Who is Christ actually for us today?", 57, 212, 213, 221, 224, 230, 232, 238–39; "Who is God?", 234; world as come of age, 57, 59, 60, 61, 64, 66, 67, 71, 77, 94, 100, 102, 104, 108, 113, 114,

153; growth of, 59; individualistic, ego-centric and inward looking, 115; and ultimate concern, 223. *See also* Bonhoeffer, Dietrich: themes

Religion als Unglaube (religion as unbelief), 69

Resistance, the, 182

resurrection, 72, 150, 199

revelational positivism, 112

revolution, 83, 84

Rieger, Julius, 156

Rilke, Rainer Maria von, 5

Robertson, Edwin, 216, 218–22

Robertson, Pat, 161

Robinson, John A. T., 75–76, 115, 166, 221; Bethge on, 131; and DB's continuity, 216; *Honest to God,* 109, 110, 111, 113, 114, 116–18, 129, 131, 229; and Lehmann, 130; Ott on, 134, 135

Roman Catholicism: DB as tempted to convert to, 156; and de Gruchy, 114; and *Index Librorum Prohibitorum,* 138; and Lutheranism, 134; and Nazi anti-Jewish strictures, 55; and orthodoxy, 163; as other, 135–36, 177; and Protestantism, 152, 154–55, 156; and relationships with Protestants

in prison and death camps, 138; in South American, 199

Rubenstein, Richard, 120

Rumscheidt, H. Martin, 66, 235

sacramentality, 151

sainthood, 144–48, 182; definition of, 147

Schleiermacher, Friedrich, 106

Schneider, Paul, 189, 190

Schoenherr, Albrecht, 85–87, 97

Schweitzer, Albert, 147, 174, 175

Second Vatican Council, 136, 138, 141, 143, 148, 152

secularism, 240; and Cox, 119; and DB, 66, 68, 72; and de Gruchy, 114, 116; and Dumas, 121; and East Germany, 92; in Great Britain, 108; growth of, 239; and Hamilton, 128; and history, 88; hopes for creative, 229; and Huntemann, 169; and Petrella, 201; respondents concerning, 60; in United States, 118–19; and West Germany, 191; and world come of age, 64, 183, 213, 232

Selby, Peter, 228–30